C'MON PAPA

ALSO BY RYAN KNIGHTON

Swing in the Hollow

Cars

(with George Bowering)

Cockeyed

RYAN KNIGHTON

C'MON PAPA

DISPATCHES FROM A DAD IN THE DARK

ALFRED A. KNOPF CANADA

PUBLISHED BY ALFRED A. KNOPF CANADA

Published in 2010 by Alfred A. Knopf Canada, a division of Random House of Canada Limited. Distributed by Random House of Canada Limited, Toronto.

Knopf Canada and colophon are registered trademarks.

www.randomhouse.ca

LIBRARY AND ARCHIVES CANADA CATALOGUING IN PUBLICATION

Knighton, Ryan
C'mon Papa / Ryan Knighton.

ISBN 978–0–307–39669–3

1. Knighton, Ryan. 2. Fatherhood. 3. Blind—Canada—Biography. 4. Fathers—Canada—Biography. 5. Authors, Canadian (English)—21st century—Biography. 6. Blind authors—Canada—Biography. I. Title.

PS8571.N55Z463 2010 362.4'1092 C2009–905229–6

Text design: CS Richardson

First Edition

Printed and bound in the United States of America

10 9 8 7 6 5 4 3 2 1

For our parents,
Kathie, Miles, Helen and Tony

CONTENTS

"Father is rather vulgar, my dear. The word Papa, besides, gives a pretty form to the lips. Papa, potatoes, poultry, prunes and prism, are all very good words for the lips; especially prunes and prism."

—Mrs. General in *Little Dorrit*

Nesting: A Prologue

• • •

Our first home was an eyesore. The kitchen alone was a pastel pink, peach, yellow and minty green sampler. The day we took possession my wife, Tracy, shaded her eyes and started to paint. I didn't. As with so many situations, I stood around and watched. Sort of.

By that point in our lives I'd been going blind—for reasons unrelated to our kitchen's colour scheme—for more than a decade. My condition is called retinitis pigmentosa. Poorly behaved genes programmed my retinas to painlessly self-destruct—very, very slowly. Seemed like they just bored themselves to death. Sometimes my blindness feels that way. Consider that Tracy had to describe hundreds of paint chips to me before picking one. I loved her for trying to include me, and felt blinder for having listened.

Inclusion is important, though. So, because I couldn't paint the kitchen, I turned my hand to a less fickle task. A row of tiles needed to let go of the wall. One morning I decided that I would help them. A surprise for Tracy, who was out procuring other hardware I wouldn't be allowed to touch.

I rummaged around the toolbox for the hammer and, having found one, or so I hoped, I wedged its claw behind the first tile, and wrenched. The tile wouldn't budge. I put more muscle to it and grunted, the way my father might. It still wouldn't give.

Some minutes later, just shy of my death, I discovered that the tile was screwed to the wall. It was the face plate of an electrical outlet. For some reason I was still breathing.

I never told Tracy what I'd done. Instead I quietly put the hammer back and resumed my post. That is, I stayed out of the way, and tried not to kick over paint cans while she finished the work. Sometimes that's all I can do. It's a hard lesson for a blind guy. When I first began to lose my sight, nobody sat me down and told me how to step aside, or how to know when stepping aside is the best contribution I can make. I still have a lot to learn about this body, even after ten years in its darkening view. I'm disabled, not adjusted.

Our ugly kitchen aside, I was at home. Cramped and worn, the apartment was ours and the building didn't leak, unlike every other Vancouver condo built in the 1990s, particularly the ones covered in stucco. That stuff is the diaper rash of real estate. At least our building's design acknowledged that Vancouver is a rainforest city on the wet West Coast, and we lived up to code. All things on the home front seemed to be fine.

Then the water came. Not rain leaking from our roof, but water from the hose our upstairs neighbour had poked into a wall to flood the infestation of baby black widow spiders she believed to be roosting there. The light fixture over our kitchen table became a shower nozzle. Our neighbour performed her pest control three times that month, determined to beat the spiders nobody else could see. Our new home had a pathological water problem and only one solution.

"How about a loft?" I asked Tracy as she searched the real estate listings.

I'd always wanted to live in an open artist's loft in an industrial park. The idea of knocking about back alleys with my white cane, all the funky acoustics of concrete and aluminum, the need to duck exposed pipes in the kitchen, the faint stink of gasoline in the freight elevator, the entire greasy package was just too delicious to be possible. But it was possible. Instead of lawn mowers in the morning, we could have forklifts. I love forklifts.

"But for how long?" Tracy said. "Wouldn't work with a family."

The subject of babies—human babies—was in the air, but we hadn't lighted on any definite plan. This was the late summer of 2003. Tracy and I had married only three months earlier. To me it still felt a bit soon to cast a kid into our scene, but, then again, we'd already been living together on and off for eight years. Conditions were good. We were in our thirties, had a mortgage and a caustic dog, owned a car that was stolen every second Friday, and had long ago mixed our books on the shelves, mine collecting dust since I'd given up print. We even had a bed with a real mattress. For my generation, when the futon goes, adulthood is upon us.

So, the case for a little Ryan or Tracy was mounting. Besides our love and dedication to one another, we were sufficiently tangled in all the mundane ways middle-class families are, not young couples who still itemize their grocery bills or write cheques to each other for long distance calls. That mundane tangling of our lives had made a nest, and now, all the nest needed was a place to call home. A son or daughter could comfortably follow, and not too far off, if we had the room. A family place.

"I dunno. I don't see why we can't start a family in a loft," I said. "Or maybe we'd just live there until, well, we're too much for it."

The two of us and a kid living in one room didn't seem all that confining to me. Until I was thirteen I shared a tiny bedroom with my two younger brothers, Rory and Mykol (his spelling, don't ask). Every night I refereed their bickering until they grew sleepy, or gave up, at which point they'd rhythmically bang their heads into their pillows. That's how they nodded off. I still have trouble falling asleep if it's too quiet, and I still don't like being alone at night.

What's more, as defined by my childhood, a home in which you can't get away from each other seemed ideal for a new family. Busy spaces were the infrastructure of my early years. My parents had bought their first house when I was three years old, a boxy three-bedroom rancher that eventually housed the six of us, a dog, a rabbit, turtles, assorted gerbils and fish, and a home office. My parents stayed in that house, in the suburb of Langley, until I was nearly thirty. They'd added to it along the way, but for most of my childhood my brothers and sister and I had little choice but to play under the kitchen sink while my mother prepped a chuck roast. We didn't want to play anywhere else, either. We could always be found under my mother's feet, or building forts with cushions and blankets next to her, making an even smaller space to play in. For a number of years, our house at the end of the cul-de-sac was at the edge of a new development, as well. We had a small backyard. On the other side of the fence was an open pasture. I'd rarely hop the fence. Over there seemed so much, and so unnecessary. The cows just stood around. It disturbed me.

So I felt I knew the virtues of being together and on top of each other. But I didn't need to make my case. Tracy was game for my loft dream, and the hunt was on. We found several that we liked, but each sold within minutes for much more than the asking price. Our choices were quickly narrowed to the one place that for some reason hadn't sold. We braced ourselves.

The building was a renovated warehouse on Vancouver's industrial east side, precisely in the kind of cyberpunk wasteland I'd always hoped to inhabit. But unlike the auto body shop across the street or the mini storage units behind, our building appeared to have been designed by the architectural firm of Fisher Price.

The building was painted in bright, blocky chunks of red and green, while the lobby sported blue and orange. Granted I couldn't differentiate between colours very well any more, but I could see enough to remember Romper Room, and to recognize the aesthetics of an ad hoc committee.

"Somebody's got a Canadian flag for curtains," Tracy said as she rang the buzzer.

"Oh no."

But the real misfortune wasn't visual. As the owner of the loft opened the most immense and foreboding steel door I've ever had the pleasure of knocking on, a toxic cloud of gas escaped. I knew this smell. It should have been choking the waiting room of the veterinary clinic where we took our pug, Cairo.

"Hi, c'mon in," the woman said. "Just finished cleaning."

I took Tracy's elbow and we shuffled into the shoebox. Despite the high ceilings and open design, I couldn't take a step without clipping my knees against boxes, kicking piles of magazines, or tagging the numerous armoires and dressers with my elbows. From what I could tell, the only other door was to the washroom. The only light came from the single wall of windows that looked out at the smeared shapes of warehouses and factories, then up to the blurry shadow of the North Shore Mountains. As the owner chatted about the apartment, I heard the Skytrain, Vancouver's monorail, hum and crawl through the near distance, and with that, with my head aching from the stink and disorientation, I was sold.

When I was a kid, after my brothers had banged their heads to sleep, my favourite thing was to listen for trains crossing through my dinky hometown. If Tracy and I had a child here, the Skytrain would be his or her version of my past. A rhyme between the sounds of our childhoods. Lineage can be more than a bloodline, and I wanted my kid, whenever he or she should arrive, to share some of the pleasures that had shaped me.

As I stood by the windows, I also realized how much I wanted the busy acoustics of a working city, not the muted, spare soundtrack of a residential street or, worse, some mini-mall lagoon. The competing noises of the world outside conjured images in my mind. I collaged a train passing, a variety of traffic, men unloading trucks and telling jokes, a rubber hammer fixing dents at Gord's Auto Body, somebody sawing next door, so many sounds, so much to see in my mind's eye. As a blind man, I'd have a view here. What did I have at our condo? Footsteps on a sidewalk. Maybe a leaf blower. Maybe the fantasy of asking the person with the leaf blower to insert the nozzle in his mouth.

In the middle of the loft was a bedroom area flanked by red brick archways, connected by what felt like a decaying medieval wall. My fingertips dragged along the mortar as I passed. For five percent down we could ride a freight elevator to a hobbit den. I was sold a second time.

I stood by the windows, revelling in the mental picture of my dream home—though labouring to breathe—when Tracy took my arm.

"It's a mess," she whispered. "There's cat litter between the floorboards. Not a little. Ditches of litter. Who knows what else."

"Just needs a vacuum," I said, and tried not to cough.

"The walls have puffy clouds on them. They're textured, too. Like frescos."

My mental picture grew more complicated.

"You mean a pattern of little clouds? Like wallpaper? The kind for a baby's room?"

"The wall is a blue sky," Tracy said. "We are in the clouds."

"That's neat, uh, right?"

But not to Tracy. A skyscape offended her simple taste, while agitating her vertigo.

"That's the washer and dryer behind the curtains," the woman said.

My mind's eye didn't know what to do. A laundry room circled by curtains?

"What's up there?" Tracy asked.

"That's a storage space above the washroom," the woman said.

"Hey, storage!" I brightened. I wanted to hear the Skytrain at night. I wanted to perch my kid on a brick wall while I tied shoelaces. "Storage is a great thing. Can't beat storage."

"It's about a three-foot-high gap above the washroom," the woman said. "A few pipes are up there, too."

"What's taped around that one?" Tracy asked. "Does it leak?"

"No," the woman said. "That's just foam around the gas line. My husband taped it there. Sometimes the kids sit up at night and bang their heads."

My mental picture blew up.

"Bang their heads against the gas line?" I said. "Above the bathroom?"

"Uh-huh. They sleep up there."

In hindsight, part of me can imagine the joy the situation must have brought those kids. Had my parents ever asked where my siblings and I would really like to sleep, we would've fought over who got the crawlspace, and who got to bunk behind the furnace or on the roof.

As Tracy and I drove home, we were too puzzled by the life of this family to make a decision.

"How do they have sex?" Tracy wondered.

"Well, okay. See, the man, first he puts his—"

"I mean there's no door. How does that work with kids?"

"Maybe they duck behind the brick wall. The parents, I mean."

"After they send their children to bed in the storage space?"

"And take away the ladder for the night."

I began to concede that maybe my dream home was not the same as my dream family home. Theirs was no place for a young family. It was curious, then, that we went back and bought it.

• • •

Tracy loves to renovate, and she's good at it, so the morning we moved in to our loft, the guys with hammers and other assorted weapons of minor destruction moved in, as well. When Tracy finished, the only things she'd kept from the original joint were the floors, the walls and the wizard's bedroom. Everything smelled new, everything felt clean and modern, or weathered and natural. When she completed arranging shelves and hiding the world in a basket or two, the acoustics opened, the light moved deeper into the room, and I could feel the air return. My remaining senses lit up and showed affection for our new home. Maybe we could make a go of it here, after all.

A monumental decision such as starting a family requires persuasive dissertations, licences, spreadsheets and field research. That's what I assumed until one night when we were lying in bed and, if I recall correctly, I asked Tracy if we were ready to have a family now, and she said sure. That was it. We didn't consult calendars, we didn't debate perils and risks, we didn't even raise the bogeyman of my blindness as a factor in parenting, or as a factor of the baby's genetic crapshoot. That night, just lying there in the comfort of the dark, the day's work done, our home a home, I suspect we'd just independently arrived at the desire for the next expression of who we are together. A baby, in and of itself, is an answer to the question why are we here in the dark, in this pleasant room, and for so many years in so many other rooms.

After that, Tracy stopped taking the pill, and every day became Christmas Eve.

ACT ONE

• • •

For Starters

The End

• • •

Neighbourhoods have an ecology. The one surrounding our cyberpunk loft made sense. The people were as eccentric as our building's colour scheme, and as busy as our industrial habitat. We had variety, biodiversity and pluralism, except for one glaring and uniform fact: nobody had kids.

Sure, one guy on the fourth floor had his daughter two days a week. But that was it. We enjoyed couples galore, but we were a kid-free Romper Room. The graffiti in the elevator was actually the work of adults. What sort would carve the word "loaf" was another matter. So, though I say we were a kid-free zone, there seemed to be exceptions. In our building we made it our pride and priority to indulge ourselves, to turn volume dials up, to erect drill presses beside our sofas, to throw raves on a Wednesday and continue them until Friday, to sleep in a medieval fantasy, and, above all, to remain stuck in the years when Judas Priest was popular. We were a plaza of Peter Pans. Me included.

The hallmark of my youth had always been recklessness. Blindness had cured much of that in my character, enforcing a more cautious person to take over. Not that I always agreed with the rules, but my body and safety demanded I live more slowly, more deliberately, and even more habitually. To that end, the neighbourhood where we'd lived before we decided to have a family had long served as an extension of my white cane. While I'd tapped around those same six blocks for ten years, living in a variety of basement suites and rooms, my mind had equally worn its own path, memorizing and building a map that I lived in. If pressed, and if nothing radical or spontaneous happened, I could have walked my old neighbourhood without a cane. Slowly, of course, and with a minor amount of pole-to-face trauma, but I could have done it. My life had a safety net of well-worn routine, and everybody knew me. Not here, though, not in Neverland's warehouse district.

Industrial parks are imagined for cars and trucks, not blind men. Grocery stores don't locate themselves within shuffling distance of a Muffler King. Here, I was a kid sleeping in the storage space of the city. Every time I came home with bruises and near-death experiences, it became clearer that I needed foam. Foam on every mailbox, signpost, chain link fence, bus bench and truck grille. Foam on every bike rack, curb, crack in the sidewalk, garbage bin and discarded pallet. It would take me years to learn this place to the degree I'd known my old neighbourhood. The work would take enough time, too, that one day I'd be forced to wrap my child in foam, for her own good. I grew to understand this with every scab and fall, and with the startle from every truck that honked me out of its path. Once, I was even moved by something more surprising and painful.

The busy intersection at Main Street and Great Northern Way was a chronic problem. I had to deal with it every time I walked to the gym, or headed into the city. Its crosswalk is likely the longest in town, and cuts across four lanes of traffic at an angle. An angle. It wouldn't give sighted folks pause, but it's hard enough to hold a straight line when you're blind, let alone hold a straight line on an angle.

One afternoon I stepped into the crosswalk, only to hear a car zip towards me. Its bumper scooped my knees and dropped me to the ground. The real surprise, though, was the specific bumper that hit me. It was a rear one. I'd been backed over at an intersection. From around a corner.

I got back on my feet, sore and alarmed, as the driver jumped out of his car. I half-expected him to walk backwards towards me.

"Wow," he said. "Gotta watch where you're going."

Sometimes I don't have the patience to explain my body. Instead I wound up and punted his tail light. It didn't shatter. My sneaker just made a soft, rubbery thud. I loathed my comfortable shoes.

"Hey," the driver said, "don't do that."

By this point other drivers were honking, cheering on the blind guy who was about to kick the crap out of a car. Backing over a blind man must've looked bad. Maybe that's why, without a word, the driver jumped back into his car and sped away. Forwards.

I shuffled back to the loft feeling both defeated and humiliated. I made it home all right, but when I got there it didn't feel safe and small. I was the resident of an outpost. I wanted to go home, back to the place I knew. My old neighbourhood was something to build upon. Familiar. A place for family.

What made my dream home so fantastic also made it impractical. The attraction was the same thing that made Dorian Gray's portrait seem like a bargain. I hadn't come here to start a family, I'd come here to live a dream of youth. But you've got to clear the nest of such things. You've got to kill your darlings to make room.

• • •

Tracy was getting ready for work one morning when she opened the bathroom door and called for me. Her voice was sharp and purposeful, a tone that indicated something was happening. We'd already dealt with a burst water pipe in the kitchen. It had flooded the loft while we were at work, and the water had run down into the closets of our neighbours. When Tracy called from the bathroom, I expected more trouble in our dream. More growing pains.

"I think I'm pregnant," she said.

"Are you sure?"

"I've taken the test twice."

"The colour, did it change?"

"It's an X or a circle."

A father for less than thirty seconds and I was already learning interesting things.

"And it's the good mark?" I asked.

I could hear the smile on her face.

When I hugged her, my body lit up with relief, as if we'd finally made it back after a long time away. Something in me was new. I was both older, and younger, than ever before.

The desire to move suddenly became urgent.

From the get-go Tracy's body handled it well. By eight weeks she still had no significant morning sickness, only a touch of nausea here and there. Not that it was easy. A tiredness crept over her that would shame narcoleptics. She could sleep anytime, anywhere, in any position. No hyperbole. I mean, we'd be at the dinner table, and I'd be in mid-sentence when I'd detect a fresh, eerie silence in the room, the kind that didn't sound to my blind man's ears like somebody listening. I'd just carry on with dinner, and hope that she'd made it to bed this time.

The need to sleep didn't curtail Tracy's drive, however. A new case of nesting was well under way. As soon as we started the hunt for a more suitable home, we lucked upon a townhouse back in our old neighbourhood. It had two bedrooms, real walls and no clouds, no protective foam necessary. Situated on a street well within my spatial memory, it seemed like a helpful and safe place to grow into fatherhood, and for Tracy to trust my body with a stroller. Then again, I wasn't sure yet how a stroller was even possible. I was already perplexed by the problem of how I would push a pram and swing my white cane at the same time. Aiming myself, the baby and the buggy would be necessary. I'm not known for my aim.

Tracy loves to move, pregnant or not, so she paced herself and organized a couple of boxes a day, or wrapped breakables in newspaper, or labelled, then alphabetized, then stacked, but only a bit at a time. Between tasks she took her vitamins, or laid her head down and snoozed beside the tape gun. Meanwhile, I talked. Or, more precisely, I talked out my anxiety.

Fatherhood, that train I heard a-comin', had stoked a few new fires of worry in my belly—nothing specific I could name yet—but luckily the move offered something else to consider, and something productive to focus my anxiety on. Basically my paternal jitters manifested in an obsession with any irrelevant object. I fixated. I worried that something might get away. Don't forget the egg whisk. Don't forget the shoehorn. That sort of thing. I suspect it was a blind guy fixation, too. Nothing was in its proper spot any more. My familiar world seemed to be disappearing all over again. The hope was that it would all somehow reappear in the next apartment, safe and unbroken, so in my mind's eye, I saw the smallest things and clung to them for hope. If my box of ear plugs made it to the next life, then surely everything else above its value and importance would arrive, including us.

To that end, I'd often lie awake at night and take inventory of our belongings, then wake Tracy and discuss what might have gone AWOL.

"Babe? You awake? Did you pack my jump rope?"

Tracy would, at most, grumble, less than pleased with my attention to detail. But I'd persist.

"I'll just go put it on the kitchen counter, okay?"

"Whatever," she'd say, barely stirring.

"Beside the cordless drill."

"Uh huh."

"Next to the meat thermometer. Can't forget that."

That's pretty much how I spent the month prior to our move. Otherwise, when I wasn't trying to keep everything in mind, I was teaching at the college.

One morning as I shaved, I was mulling over that day's lesson plan. Even though I instruct undergraduates how to compose essays or, at the very least, to appreciate a nice sentence, I have yet to be persuaded that the world suits anything called a "thesis statement." You just don't find them anywhere, or at least I've yet to polish off anything that would prompt me to say, "Quick, Tracy! Come check out my thesis statement! I think it's got a real handle on things!"

As I mulled over what to say on the subject, Tracy appeared at the bathroom door, smelling of perfume, ready to go to work. She spoke the first words of the day. Our thesis statement.

"I'm bleeding."

She sounded panicky, and confused. She'd almost phrased it as a question.

"I'm sure it's normal. I mean, isn't that normal?"

So many things about Tracy's body were changing that I couldn't tell what was to be expected any more.

"No," she said, "Bleeding now isn't normal. It isn't good at all. The books don't say anything good about it."

"I'm sure it's fine," I said. "Let's just call the doctor and make an appointment, just to be certain. But I'm sure it's . . ."

Her fingers were already dialling.

By early afternoon we'd seen our doctor, we'd gone for an ultrasound, and we'd learned that the baby was gone. No heartbeat could be found. That fast, that blunt. That final. Maybe there had never been a heartbeat. We were only eight weeks pregnant. Most people—our friends and co-workers—didn't even know.

Though miscarriage is not the final story of our family, it is the context in which my fatherhood, and Tracy's motherhood, was born. We began in exile and flux. A painful and anxious uncertainty tempered the joy of taking the next step in our lives. Could I be a father? Would I? Should we? What were our bodies telling us, if anything? We had moved into parenthood, only to be kicked out again. Now we lived between homes, between grief and hope, life and death, restless and, to a degree, lost.

As soon as we returned home from the hospital, our old life tried to pick up where it had left off. When at your most vulnerable, reality has a way of punishing you with its banality. Are you hungry? No. But can you turn the radio on? Sure. Did you arrange the moving insurance?

In one day our pregnancy had become a parenthesis. An aside. Now closed. Still, we crawled into bed that night and slept with a question between us. How do we begin, again?

I guess you have to clear the nest. Let your darlings go. Some, to the ground.

• • •

Somewhere outside a busy Vancouver grocery store, Tracy yanked me around another bike rack. How's a fella going to start a family if he keeps castrating himself against sidewalk amenities? That was my thought, when I heard a ringing. I'm sure a dozen other people reached into their pockets, but it was Tracy's phone.

I couldn't piece together who she was talking to, but somebody wanted to see us. Sooner rather than later, it seemed. When she hung up, she paused for a moment, then made a puzzled sound.

"That was the doctor's office," she said. "They asked to see us this afternoon."

"Why?"

"A follow-up appointment. See how I'm doing, I guess. How we're doing"

It sounded reasonable and caring, but unlikely. Doctors,

in my experience, don't have the time or resources to personally call up their patients. Definitely not to request a second post-miscarriage chat. Not a chance. Tracy's pause and puzzled sound indicated that she was thinking the same thing. Not even a month had passed. We weren't supposed to try to become pregnant again quite so soon, we already knew that. What more could there be to discuss? It's not like we needed a doctor's nudge about planned parenthood.

To this day, whenever I hear the page of a magazine flip, I think of pelvic exams. We were in a waiting room and waiting for one. I listened to Tracy thumb through *Marie Claire* while I eavesdropped on the receptionists and the other patients, all of them flipping other magazines, perhaps readying other pelvises for other examinations. I'd heard the same scene the day we confirmed we were pregnant, and again when we waited in the hospital for a D & C to remove any residual tissue from the miscarriage. It makes you think differently about the magazine industry and its audience.

When it was finally our turn, and the doctor appeared, she was quick and to the point. The exam began, then it was over. The doctor rolled back on her little stool. She read through Tracy's file as she spoke. I could hear pages flipping. Maybe the doctor was brushing up on the new spring fashions, too. Maybe she had a pelvic exam scheduled for herself.

"You're feeling well?" she asked.

"As well as can be expected," Tracy said.

"And you?" the doctor asked.

"Me?" I said. "I'm okay if she's okay."

Pages flipped. The doctor offered no reply. I didn't like her response. I'd set her up, but she hadn't reassured me that I was allowed to feel all right since Tracy was fine, too.

"The tissue that we removed during the D & C was biopsied," the doctor said. "It's a standard procedure. The results indicate that the pregnancy was actually molar. Typically we'd have seen that on the ultrasound, but—do you know what a molar pregnancy is?"

We blanked.

"I should clarify that yours was what we consider a partial molar," added the doctor.

Good, I thought. Things were only half as bad as they seemed. Or partially as bad.

"Basically," the doctor continued, "in your case the egg was fertilized by two sperm."

Tracy and I had the same thought, but just one of us said something about twins.

"No," the doctor said, "Unfortunately the chromosomes are doubled, and that causes the problem. It creates these cells, these molar cells. We intervened in your miscarriage very early. That's possibly why we didn't see the presence of these cells on the ultrasound, too."

"Why is it called a molar pregnancy?" I asked. "As in teeth?"

The doctor laughed. This hadn't been my intention.

"It has nothing to do with teeth, at least not as far as I know," she said.

Medical metaphors are perplexing. Often they don't make clear pictures in a person's mind. Like most people, I suspect, I like to have a picture in my mind. Of most things, at least. Ever had an episode of the sitcom *Full House* described to you? I rest my case.

"What does molar mean, then?" I asked. "Where does it come from?"

"You know," the doctor said, "I can't honestly say. I think it's—well—no, I can't say I know why. Good question."

I like to figure these things out, so I pressed.

"Well, what about a mole? Is it something to do with the cells and how they behave? Are they, you know, mole-like?"

"Could be."

She didn't sound convinced. Not of anything other than she had a metaphor-fixated patient.

"But there must be some reason they call it that. I mean, why would you use a term like molar if—"

I could feel that Tracy was kicking me in her mind with an imaginary steel-toed boot, telling me to can it. I let the metaphor go. If a molar pregnancy meant something could be burrowing, I doubted Tracy wanted to know.

That's when my gal cut through semantics to the real stuff.

"So what does this mean?" she said.

The doctor seemed relieved to be back on scientific turf, away from its language.

"Yes," she said, and clapped Tracy's file shut, "what it means is this: we need you to have a few blood tests over the next couple of weeks. That's all. We watch the growth hormone levels in your body. Since you're no longer pregnant, they should go down."

"And if they don't?" Tracy asked. Her voice was stone.

"If some of the molar cells remain, and if they're dividing, the hormone levels will rise. More there, more to feed, see?"

For once I could see. What she was describing was a cellular infestation. I'm surprised nobody had worded it that way.

Tracy sat in a chair opposite me. She was just far enough away that I couldn't reach for her hand, or pat her thigh, or offer something, without drawing attention to the gesture.

She's proud and reserved. I decided to let her be, to protect at least that much.

"What we need to do is take some blood today and take some next week, to monitor that your levels are going down. Typically they do."

"And if they don't," Tracy asked. Her stone voice had a quiver now. Earthquake.

"Not to worry," the doctor said. A flash of teeth caged her words. "There are a variety of options. We'll visit those in the exceptional circumstance that we need to. It is treatable. Really, it's very unlikely, though."

"How unlikely?" I asked.

"The chances are very, very remote. About five percent."

"And how common is a molar pregnancy?" I asked.

"Oh, maybe one in a thousand."

Numbers of this order are intended to reassure people, but I had yet to experience much relief. Here was a physician telling us that we'd already gone from the wrong side of a typical one-in-fifteen chance of miscarriage, to the short straw on a one-in-a-thousand chance of a cellular disorder. Now we were crapshooting a one-in-twenty chance of something else. It seemed to me that every time we participated in something rare, our chances of getting rarer increased.

I'd like to believe there's safety in numbers, but there isn't. Put it this way. If you have a one-in-a-million chance of dying in a plane crash, statistics would definitely be on your side if you planned to wear a bear costume and ride a unicycle to your seat. That should be better odds of survival than a parachute, right? I mean, what are the chances of a person in a bear costume, one with a unicycle in the overhead storage bin, dying in a plane crash? As rare as they get.

If numbers really worked that way, rather than waiting for Tracy's ninety-five percent chance of those pernicious little cells suffering a hormone famine, we should have been out pricing unicycles after we left the doctor's office. Another health insurance, you might say.

Two blood tests later, we learned that Tracy's hormone levels were rising, not diminishing. Her body thought she was pregnant, but she wasn't. Cells were dividing. We went into full alarm. We were also officially beyond the realm of our general practitioner's skill. An appointment was made for us with a specialist. He was, from what Tracy told me, a tidy and charming young man whose hands gestured as he spoke, his gestures made with equal articulation.

I don't remember what was said first, or how we directed our small talk to some hard information about what options we faced. I do recall, however, that we rocketed to the fact there was one option and only one.

"Chemotherapy," he said. "You'll need to begin treatment right away."

A placenta is a miraculous and peculiar creation. It effectively behaves like a benign cancer, attaching itself to a woman's system, feeding off it, and growing. But, being benign, a placenta is also programmed to detach. To destroy itself, unlike a cancer. These cells, these molar cells, were related to the placenta. They didn't know when to quit, though, and so they grew, and fed, and grew, and if left to themselves would spread to the brain and lungs. Not cancer, but cancer-like. Lethal, albeit vulnerable.

"I would guess it will take a treatment or two," the gynecologist said. "The sooner the better. The less we're treating, the less treatment necessary."

Two weeks later, the morning of Tracy's first treatment, we called a taxi. When the yellow blur pulled up to our house, I was saddened, struck by a sharp, then deflating sensation. I couldn't drive my wife to the cancer clinic. She'd be in no condition to drive herself home, either, so here we were, inviting a stranger along, into a place that had no room for strangers. I would have given my hearing to be able to drive that day.

In the back seat we were surrounded by bags. Our arms were filled with Tracy's pillows, some home-cooked food, books, needlepoint, Sudoku collections, and a portable DVD player, among other things. She was only going overnight, but the intensity of what she would experience asked for more distraction and comfort than a week away from home in any other circumstances. As I shut the cab door, I gave the driver instructions.

"We're going to the BC Cancer Agency," I said. "Do you know where that is?"

He did. He'd delivered blood there before. As we drove, all of us silent, Tracy caught the cabbie's eyes as he glanced into his rear-view mirror. He was looking at me. His eyes were filled with sympathy—Tracy said others would do this, too. The same look was visited upon me by folks at the cancer agency lobby, as well as the families and friends of other patients who passed us in the hallway as we searched for the nurse's station. Everybody saw a blind, bald man and assumed there was cancer behind my hairstyle. Perhaps behind my blindness.

But I was glad when Tracy told me about the looks. I decoyed attention from her. I could do so little for her now, so I was happy to have the job of a red-herring patient. I absorbed the pity for her. It was one less toxicity, maybe.

In a narrow room, at the end of a long, disinfected hallway, we were guided to a bed by a chipper and quick nurse. Tracy shared the room with a Chinese woman who occupied the only other bed, half-hidden behind a curtain. The woman's nurse and her family were circled around the bed, and in a flap about something. *The Price Is Right* blasted from the tiny TV above them. Tracy changed and climbed into her own bed, then began arranging her things for the overnight stay.

Soon the picture of what was happening next door came into focus. As Tracy unpacked, I listened to the next-bed woman's family. They struggled to translate a nurse's questions and instructions. Between short bursts of Chinese, the woman moaned in pain. The room smelled stale and heavy. Sour and hot. It would only thicken over the day. This was breakfast time. This was a fresh new start.

Our chipper nurse finished taking Tracy's vitals, and began to insert an IV drip into her wrist. This would be the delivery mechanism for the chemo. But the needle seemed to be giving some trouble, then a lot of trouble. The nurse was on her third attempt at finding a vein when the situation next door reached a boiling point. The neighbouring nurse was flustered, as was the family. The nurse spoke slow and loud.

"Has she been vomiting, or experiencing diarrhea?"

The family spoke among themselves. The woman moaned.

"Vomiting?" The nurse repeated. "Tummy upset?"

"Maybe I'll have to try the other arm," Tracy's nurse said. "This one won't seem to take."

She pricked Tracy again, where four previous holes were already abandoned and swollen.

A wave of panic broke from the family around the next bed.

"No!" the Chinese woman's nurse shouted. "No getting

up. You must tell her to stay in bed. She kept getting up last night and—no, down, in bed, please!"

"She go bathroom," a family member said. "She was bathroom. She is gone."

Folks scrambled for a bedpan. Tracy tried to focus her attention somewhere else. Her own end of the room wasn't a viable option. The nurse was on her sixth attempt at finding a vein.

"We need to get you to relax," she said, both frustrated and apologetic. "When our bodies are stressed, they defend themselves. Veins dive down further from the surface. It's a form of self-protection. Yours are pretty defensive."

The chaos next to us focused on arranging the family around the woman to help lift her into a wheelchair, to take her to a bathroom. It wasn't happening, though, because the woman was too frail, or too upset. Tracy was upset, too. Her bruised and bleeding arms were wrapped in thick hot towels in an attempt to coax her veins back to the surface. She said she felt like a perversion of the Michelin man.

Around the time Tracy's IV finally took, a woman approached the bed. She had a thick Scottish accent, comforting like good stew, and I caught a broad glint of light from her chest. I thought it could be an amulet, not a stethoscope. This was Tracy's oncologist. She'd prepared the day's cocktail, and was here to prepare Tracy for the twelve-hour infusion.

I was wary of this doctor from the get-go, although I had no reason to be. My fears attached themselves to the oncologist's necklace. Why did she wear an amulet? I didn't want the person responsible for curing my wife to also dabble in the powers of symbols and magic tokens. I felt the same conflict about the airline mechanic who told me the Big Bang never happened, since it wasn't spoken of in the Bible. Who wants to fly in a plane maintained by a denier of physics? I had a bad feeling. A protective, bad feeling.

The Chinese woman wept. Her family consoled her.

Like me, this woman's family was here, but exiled from what was happening inside someone they loved. Our bodies enforce a remoteness from one another, a barrier that we spend our lives trying to break through in a variety of ways. We send our voices across a room. A look. We ask for long embraces. We reserve the physical intimacy of touch, taste and smell for so few. For two people lucky enough, a baby bridges and binds the molecular gap between them. We grow close, as they say. Atomic.

Perhaps Tracy's oncologist, alert to the despair and suffering from the next bed, understood that we were struggling not to see it as our story, too, and how this chapter could end. Whatever cued her, I can say for certain she then gave us the best and most difficult request we'd had from any medical practitioner, albeit a counter-intuitive prescription.

"Let me ask that you do one thing for me, and for yourselves, " she said. "I don't want you to identify with any of the other patients here."

She let the admonition sing for a moment before qualifying her advice.

"You are not them. You don't have cancer. Chemotherapy just happens to be the effective therapy for molar tissue. It will work, one hundred percent. You will not lose your hair, you will not need radiation or surgery, and when it is over and you are well, you can go on to have a healthy family. I'll say it again if you like—you will be fine, no question."

With that, just before Tracy's infusion began, I remember an incredible lift. For the first time in all of this, a doctor had given us some certainty, and its specific kind of relief. Chemo would be hell on Tracy, no question, but she would be fine. Little, but enough. Few can give that much.

Whenever the doctor came around, she was so casual, cheerful. Certain. Her amulet was bright and cut through the smear of my eyes, and I was happy to catch it.

We reminded ourselves of what the doctor had said whenever things got hard, whenever doubts crept in. A child was possible. We'd have to wait a year before we could try again, to ensure the cells did not return, but that's all. A year's down time. The incubation of a pause. It felt like a promise, if we kept it in that light.

The suggested couple of treatments swelled to three, then tipped to four as Tracy's levels continued to rise. But the amulet also continued to catch light whenever it came around to see how she was doing. After that, five treatments seemed to be the magic number. Then it was revised to six. Finally her levels peaked and began their decline. We hung on to science and certainty, the clarity of the words. "You'll be fine," I reminded my gal. "Just a little more to go."

During her first day of treatment, I sat beside Tracy, we talked, we watched movies and, when she was tired, she slept and I listened to her breathing. Sometimes she'd ask me to get her juice, so I'd open my cane and tap around until I found a nurse who could guide me to a vending machine, or I'd grope about to find one myself on the next floor, or follow noises to the cafeteria for change. In the elevator, if I was alone, I felt nervous and urgent. I had to get back fast, be faster. Be there. Not get lost.

After what seemed an eternity of hallways and closets and wrong turns, I offered the juice to Tracy's outstretched hand. My own small amulet. My own token of apology for feeling I'd done this to her. Then she restarted the DVD, told me what was going on, and sipped her drink, nursing the gap between us. Us and a family we'd imagined.

Ape, Chicken, Dad

• • •

The townhouse that we moved into seemed labyrinthian, especially after dwelling in our loft's single room. I had a complicated new space to memorize, so I spent the first few days shuffling from room to room, feeling for light switches, counting stairs, pacing the shape, and trying to plug my fingers into wall sockets. The main attraction when we'd bought our place had been the two large bedrooms. One, which would have been the baby's, was easily the most generous and pleasant. On the second floor, facing east, the bay window siphoned as much sunlight each morning as the space could hold. The baby's room was brilliant, empty and cruel.

We didn't know what to do with it. My desk and office needed to go somewhere—my scribbliotheque, as we called it—but instead I chose to bury myself in the basement. Tracy understood. I set up shop beside the washing machine, while a spare bed went into the baby's room. Winter coats filled the closet. Tattered dog toys collected in the corner, a worn chair sat by the window. Everything went unused.

We made fresh starts of other kinds. Tracy switched corporate jobs, crafting language for a new CEO, and I penned a few bits and bobs that made me laugh. I played guitar badly on the couch and, once in a while, we walked new neighbourhoods and ate new foods in foreign cities, figuring it would be harder to up and travel about the world so casually when, one day, a baby arrived. This wasn't just leisure, mind you. This was strategy. Our own psy-ops against time. Indulging in such things—things that weary new parents beg you to revel in while you can—reinforced our hope of a baby's inevitability. Good thing we're doing this now before we've got kids, eh? Yep, things are gonna change in a year when we can try again, right? Best to enjoy movies and reading the paper while we've still got the cognitive power to do so. A baby—our baby—will mandate a prolonged sleep deprivation. One day a baby will arrive. We knew that. We believed that and behaved as if it was an assumption predicating our lives, as if the baby was just on a plane heading home from its own holiday abroad.

One year. That's a hell of a long and dangerous measure for my eyes. The last functional speck of sight that remained in my right one could go at any time. My sight disappears in landslides. I don't lose a bit every day, like a slow dimming of the lights. Rather, I'll be looking at an apple in a grocery store one day when suddenly it seems as if a few of the lights just burned out overhead and, ain't that something, a chunk of the apple's periphery just disappeared, like an island that somehow sank deeper into the ocean. A radical change like that happens suddenly, then nothing happens for months, or perhaps even for a year or two. There's no predicting, but when a slide comes, a bit of the shoreline around my last island of clarity dissolves into a Vaseline sea. Each time was a big change despite losing so little. Big. That's the irony. The less you have, the more you have to lose.

What worried me most in the year we had to wait was that I had so little sight left that I could easily say goodbye to it before I got the chance to glimpse the tiniest bit of my son or daughter. I wanted to piece together what I could of that face before that opportunity was taken from me for good. A year of waiting could disappear my baby from me before it had even arrived.

What can you do, though? For a year I watched the calendar, half a number and half a letter at a time, always glad to see at least that much. I clung to its promise. The calendar said there would be a future.

There were other, more productive distractions, too. Daddyhood preparation worked well. Often I stared at the latest fatherly primers, half a letter at a time. The rest of the book's cover, my hand, wrist, and the room beyond, all resembled a lively smear of light and line. Of course I could have picked up one of the few shortened audio book titles, but that struck me as a crappy first move into parenting. What does it say about a man if he reads up on fatherhood in an abridged format? Can't be good, especially if he has a year to kill.

For the most part I was stuck with print. No problem, I would enlist help, maybe a buddy could read to me. Unfortunately Tracy already had enough of her own reading to do, most of it by zealots who tub-thumped about what good mothers do and don't do. Some say to enjoy a glass of wine during pregnancy, others would torch you for it. Every type of food seemed to make it onto somebody's danger list, even salad. Tracy's reading had turned into something more like criminal litigation than an afternoon with a book.

My friend Brian gave me a hand one day. He helped me study up on becoming a dad. All the chapters in the first fatherhood guide we picked up were lessons imparted by sports metaphors. "The Handoff" was about how to hold and pass the baby to my wife, and "The Huddle" was about how to communicate with her about the baby, which itself may have been called "The Win," a child being the living consequence of having "Scored." After reading that much I was glad I couldn't see. I was already blind. I didn't need to become an idiot, too.

The sad fact is that, as shown above, most of these books assume a new father has sore knuckles from dragging them on the ground most of his life, and has a hairline that begins an inch above his one eyebrow. Nevertheless, my studies continued.

In another book I was instructed to paste favourite photos of Tracy, myself and the baby to our child's car seat. The idea was that the baby could enjoy the pictures during a car ride, while also learning to recognize family. An educational moment, as they call it. Letting the baby look out the window at the actual world couldn't compare. Could I argue?

But I must be lacking the necessary degree in physics, or maybe I need a refresher in the basics of sighted reality to understand the instructions here. How the hell is the baby supposed to look at pictures she's sitting on? Are baby necks really that pliable? Excuse me while I scratch my hairy forehead in confusion.

It got worse. The next chapter described a web of dental floss I was to knit about the car's interior. The floss would connect back and forth, up and down, around any available space in the back seat, in order to attach a constellation of clothes pegs that could then hold—you guessed it—family photos. There was no explanation why anybody, fathers in particular, should do this. I can only guess that the baby would get tired of wedging his head behind his own spine to look at the pictures pasted there.

The dental net had one safety application, I suppose. At least if the little rascal somehow unbuckled herself to get a better look at a picture, a web of floss would keep her from being launched through the windshield. Must be hard for a parent to pay attention to the road when he's chronically wrenched around and updating the family car seat.

I finally gave the abridged audio books a go. The selection was slender, and so I started with what was available and easy to find. Bill Cosby's anecdotal wisdom arrived in the mail. As long as his book didn't require new dads to invest in geometrically busy sweaters, I was game to listen.

I survived ten minutes or so, then shut it off after the chapter about how Cosby taught his son a lesson by taking him out to the barn for a drubbing. Fat Albert's parenting methods were as dated as the cassette tapes he recorded them on.

Ultimately, most books for dads didn't make me long to have my sight back. In fact, from all indications, sighted dads are a dangerous lot who should have all glue sticks, barns and dental floss kept out of reach.

As the year went by, I not only grew a bit blinder, but also more and more confused by my studies about what a father is, and how I could be one of them.

In a Turkish restaurant one afternoon over beer and lamb, I was chewing, considering burying myself alive for a magazine article, when Tracy casually interrupted my death trip musings.

"I think I'm pregnant," she said.

We'd literally been clear from our year's pause for a month. She'd been off the pill for just as long, and because I'd been travelling so much to promote my memoir, we'd only been together once in that month. I'm a keener and all, but this exceeded over-achiever standards.

I nursed my beer and waited for the surge of adrenaline to dilute.

"You think you're pregnant," I repeated, "or you are, you know, pregnant?"

"I am."

My skull rattled from whatever spazzed in there. My mind. Not a mind, but what was formerly a mind. Now it was just a chicken with no head. I didn't know what to say. I couldn't keep up, let alone respond with words. I needed to catch the chicken.

"—but you might not be," I tried.

"No, I'm pretty sure I am."

"You're pretty—?"

"I'm sure."

Tracy's joy was clear. Mine was in me somewhere, but hard to find for the noise and flap of the chicken. I just felt chicken. So, I expressed that feeling as best I could.

"No, you're not," I said.

The words surprised me as much as they surprised Tracy.

A baby is, by design and delivery, a surprise. You can plan to have one, get to work on that plan, prepare yourselves, foster encouraging conditions of body and environment, try under a full moon, check body temperature and consult the calendar, try again, one more's the trick, then say it's going to happen soon, now, I can just tell, something feels different, I think something this way cometh. But all the effort and planning and trying that can go into a pregnancy doesn't mitigate the fact that when you find out one day that you and your beloved are, indeed, in a family way, you're surprised. Then, irony of all ironies, for nine months after that surprise you say you're "expecting." What you're expecting, of course, will be an even bigger surprise, though apparently you're expecting it.

People, including those who are planning a family, react to the surprise in different and interesting, sometimes inexplicable ways. Certainly I was no exception, and I couldn't understand my dunderheaded response. We'd wanted to have a baby for so long, why the immediate denial when I was suddenly brought to the edge of fatherhood?

Maybe it was, in part, a genetic thing. When I was seven years old, my younger brother, Rory, was all of two, and my other brother, Mykol, had just completed one full year in this puzzling world. That was enough for Ma. She had two in diapers, three of us underfoot. We had just enough seat belts in the car. Both my father and my mother were happy with their brood, and were done.

So, Ma loaded us all on her bicycle one afternoon—does motherhood naturally impart such profound powers of engineering?—and we made a visit to our family doctor, a funny, crunchy old country gentleman who, upon seeing my toddler's wobble, described me as having my feet on backwards. Ma was here to finalize the arrangements for a tubal ligation, the preliminary blood work already having been ordered. Dr. Gillam had Ma's results, and began the appointment by congratulating her. She was pregnant.

Of course she was thrilled, but it took a moment for her to let that feeling surface and express itself. First, instead, she punched Dr. Gillam in the face.

Despite Ma declaring "No!" several times after the punch, roughly eight months later my sister Erin was born. My parents had always wanted a girl among their boys, and so the baby's refreshing new pronoun was an extra surprise. Sometimes I still affectionately call Erin by a more accurate name, if not a good wrestling handle—the Error.

As indicated by her fists, Ma is nothing if not direct. I am too, in my own way. Denial is pretty direct.

Tracy tried to reach me again. "I'm pregnant," she said. "Really."

The chicken spoke.

"No, you're not," it said again, cheerful and confident.

The silence sang between us.

Tracy seemed to take this response as both naïve and stupid on my part, both of which were right. She was even somewhat amused by it, as if observing a strange animal in its habitat.

I continued to smile, certain of my position, patient even, as if correcting somebody who'd just told me that the Eagles had made a serious musical contribution to Western civilization and that I should just give them another listen. I resumed enjoying my lamb.

"And how would you know if I'm pregnant or not?" Tracy said.

"You're not because . . ." I stretched to peek over the end of the equation. "Because you can't be."

The chicken and I smiled again, self-satisfied, and triumphantly sipped our beer. At this rate we could pen our own fatherhood manual.

Ironically, Tracy and I had been engaged in a battle with time and age on various fronts, but now that I was faced with the prospect of actually becoming a father—locked in the transformation of that moment—I denied it for just a few beats longer, and then a few more. Just to buy more time. The very thing we didn't want in the first place. I had accepted our first pregnancy so easily, but this time I had fear. Things can go wrong. We knew that too well.

If I parse that moment in the restaurant, so much was happening, and I doubt if I'm the only father who has tried to buy some time with a little denial. The reason, when made most plain, is simple. When I learned Tracy was pregnant this time around, I stalled, playing for time to rehearse every possible situation in the future, and to gauge in each case my ability, or inability, to be the kind of husband and father it demanded. I had enough fear to do that and it all came to the surface this time. I suppose it's not unlike dying. I saw my life flash before me, but it was the life I was about to live. How will I teach her colours? What will I say when he bangs up his mother's car? How will I know he's not making faces at me as I chew him out? One day she'll be embarrassed that her father walks into sandwich boards on the street. How will I make it okay for her? Maybe disbelief would buy me a little more time, just enough to plan a life. I wanted to be a good father, a perfect father, and so I wanted to be ready. All the time in the world might just be enough to get it right. They serve all the time in the world at Turkish restaurants, don't they?

Truth is, of course, that Tracy was pregnant and I knew nothing. Nothing except that I also secretly believed I'd already botched it for us. Here's why.

On the unbelievably lucky conception-night in question, I'd just returned from a trip to Germany. There, among other things, I'd rediscovered the pleasures of chain smoking. Just to add to the chemistry, the last night of my trip found me in an old East Berlin punk club, face down at the bottom of my first bottle of absinthe. The next morning I crawled on a plane back to Vancouver and somehow made it home with what few brain cells remained, still feeling the toxicity of my European adventures, more a sack of poison than a man of flesh. Yes, I know smoking is bad for me, and absinthe actually isn't one of the four food groups, but somehow Europe made it all seem so, I don't know, vital.

My chicken was afraid of a baby that would arrive in this world smelling like an ashtray with petroleum notes of absinthe. What's more, the baby would suffer either nineteenth-century artistic genius or the temperament of an East Berlin nihilist.

The situation gets worse. Within a day of my toxic return I felt very, very odd. It was evening, and Tracy and I left a café, crossing the street. As we stepped off the curb, my sensorium went on the fritz. I turned my head to listen for oncoming traffic, but my hearing seemed to hang back in the direction my ears had just canvassed. I turned my head again, and again my ears were still sort of listening, or at least reporting, what they'd picked up before I turned away. It was dizzying, like the experience of tracers when your gaze drags the light, only these were auditory tracers. The synch between my senses and my movements was fried. I was fried.

"What's wrong?" Tracy said.

I panicked, uncertain how she knew what was going on inside my body. Then I realized that I'd been standing curbside and pivoting my head back and forth, experimenting with the trippy acoustic effect, my head behaving more like a satellite dish looking for a signal than a man listening for traffic.

I explained what I was feeling. Tracy couldn't speculate any causes other than those I'd already considered: jet lag, physical exhaustion from my trip, absinthe residuals and everything great about East Berlin. I set the feeling aside and chalked it up to something temporary.

But the feeling didn't pass. It grew more intense. By the next day I was in full fever and finding the air in my lungs damp and heavy, as if my insides had shrunk. My body hung like concrete, and my colour matched.

Turns out I had been incubating a case of pneumonia, and now it was in full bloom.

Tobacco, absinthe and pneumonia, the perfect conditions to bring a new life into this world. Surprise. After all the fret of the previous year, a holy trinity of toxins was my first fatherly contribution to the life of our child.

I should have been pasting photos in the car.

Let's Play Math

• • •

We drove to Chinatown for our first ultrasound. We'd been through this process once before, of course, during the earlier pregnancy, so I knew what to expect. Didn't seem to matter, though. Yet again I was filled with a giddy exhilaration that I was about to see something I knew damn well I wouldn't see. You'd think I'd learn.

As Tracy scanned for parking, I surveyed my memories of the neighbourhood. They imparted a good feeling. The cramped and sweaty clinic was near a bar Tracy and I had frequented years earlier on Friday nights, the two of us dancing and drinking, flirting while the floor hopped with skinny retro-men in pompadours and wing tips. Across the street from the clinic stood a congested emporium where we'd spent a day sorting through bamboo baskets and Asian vases, some of which decorated the tables at our wedding reception. Tracy parked the car and we walked past the narrowest building in the world. Inside, three years earlier, Jack Chow's Insurance Company sold us our marriage licence. Chinatown had been good to us. I hoped its ultrasound clinic wouldn't be an exception.

The technician seated me in a chair in the corner of a softly lit room. The only discernible feature was a big screen that looked to me like a window view of, well, colours. Tracy lay down on a bed. In a soft voice the nurse explained that she had to goop up Tracy's belly to allow the ultrasound wand to slide about with greater ease. The smallest movements jerked the picture across the screen, setting off a kaleidoscope in my eyes. Not that the effect was anything new to me. Even if she could have conjured a studio portrait of our child, to me the baby would continue to look like a salad. But I remained hopeful I would recognize something, some sort of baby shape.

The nurse found her spot and went to work, checking angles and clicking the computer mouse, snatching images. Tracy could see the baby, and she welled with the feelings only such a first sight can impart. What ignited in me was a joy by proxy. I bathed in the knowledge that Tracy was seeing the baby for us. It looked like a flash of light, she said. The tiniest life. Nothing more than a heartbeat. That was my first sight. Not the flash of heartbeat itself, but those words, that description, and what it resembled in my mind. I felt happy for Tracy, excited to be a father, proud for the three of us, and cheated of the experience.

Though I haven't seen my own face in nearly a decade, I sometimes believe, albeit subconsciously, which means stupidly, that this time things will be different, that this one image will somehow steal its way through the fog. Needless to say, the baby was no exception. It remained an abstraction. An idea reconstituted from Tracy's description. A flash. I thrilled in front of the computer screen, hunting for a heartbeat's shape, but seeing nothing. I could feel my desire caged and pressed against the bars, wanting to experience the freedom and immediacy of sight. It does a funny thing to a blind guy. I'm there, but always with me is a feeling that part of my being is withheld. Denied access to the real. Even a pixelated version of the real.

A few clicks and a few pictures later, our technician said that the baby seemed fine. Relief flooded through me. So far, everything was where it ought to be, and doing what it ought to do.

We stepped back outside into the sun and the smell of vegetables and fish. I warned Tracy to be careful at every curb, and swept my cane ahead for both of us. She didn't need me to do this of course, but I wanted to, for her and the baby. Because all was well, she seemed more fragile than when we'd walked into the clinic.

Immediately, the bureaucratic flow of medical information and appointments began. The next person we went to see was not our family doctor or an obstetrician, but my old high-school girlfriend, Andrea.

Andrea and I had been in home room together in grade eleven. We'd been in drama club together, too. Then we'd been everywhere together, and during the two or three weeks we'd held hands in the cafeteria, or on a bench in the smoke pit behind the library—the free hand that wasn't holding our respective smokes, that is—during those two or three weeks, puppy love had bestowed upon us its promises of an amorous eternity. Bryan Adams sang about this sort of feeling. It was syrupy and naïve. Andrea had even framed some of my poetry and hung it on her bedroom wall. My haiku, "Which One of You Built the Bomb?" was featured most prominently. As I say, we lasted about two weeks, which is longer than most people can actually survive on syrup, or listen to Bryan Adams without inserting a bread knife between their ears. I can't honestly remember why we broke up, or for whom we broke up, as the case probably went, but I do remember feeling like the world had ended as I walked home from her house for the last time. That angst endured, despite my best teenaged efforts to nurse it, for a whole week. Then, somehow, as if nothing had ever happened, Andrea and I resumed our prior friendship. Teenagers are good at moving on. Perhaps there's just not enough past to get stuck in.

It was a good thing we'd kept in touch after high school, albeit sporadically, because now, nearly fifteen years later, my high-school sweetheart was going to be our midwife.

A friend of ours had recommended Andrea's midwifery clinic, not knowing she and I had dated. Occasionally Tracy and I ran into Andrea or her sisters on the street, and so, as our prospective midwife, Andrea would bring that comforting element of familiarity. It wasn't like I said to Tracy one morning, "Hey, wanna meet my old girlfriend for a pelvic exam?" In fact it was Tracy who urged me to pick up the phone and make an appointment for us.

When I say it was a midwifery clinic, some—particularly men, myself included—might have a picture in mind of something medieval, or witchy, or, worse, hippie-dippy. The word "midwife" no doubt conjures thoughts of cats and the Inquisition, or those stern British matriarchs with a fetish for boiling water and fresh towels. Blindness has saved me from being further stupefied by television's blue light and two-dimensional universe. Still, the midwifery connotations linger, and to be honest, I was all for the idea of a midwife but had only the vaguest idea what a midwife was, or did. Doesn't a midwife mean home birth? Did we have enough towels for that, and confidence?

I didn't know, for instance, that they are conferred—at least where we live—the legal status of a general practitioner, and are even covered by medical insurance. They are specialists and have hospital privileges, can prescribe drugs as necessary and order tests, and are likely more versed in the contemporary scientific literature about pregnancy and labour than most family physicians. Pregnancy and childbirth are a midwife's business, pure and simple. I was for any model that made Tracy feel hopeful and, dare I say, safe. Enough medical threats and procedures dog pregnancy that the system made our happiness feel like a state of vulnerability. You know where that leads. A happy person is subject to the law of physics that every action has an equal, opposite reaction. The cosmos, in other words, is governed by irony.

But check this out. More perks abound. As if a midwife wasn't enough, Tracy would have not just one of them, or two, but three. A private medical team, a board of labour directors, a platoon of baby catchers—and they would even provide postpartum care at home. House calls. Who the hell makes house calls in the twenty-first century? Midwives do. Blind husbands, at least the ones who agree not to drive, are even happier for it.

The hazy idea of something Gothic lingered in the back of my mind when we first visited Andrea's clinic. Something from Victorian novels, maybe. But when we opened the door, any stereotype vanished. Everything "clinical" about the clinic itself disappeared, too, wiped away by the tinkle of a quaint little bell as the front door closed behind us. We sat down to wait on a cushy sofa. No Muzak needled my ears, no easy listening of any kind. The walls were warm colours and two new parents sat on another couch tickling their infant. Opposite us stood a modest library, a bookshelf with videos and tomes about everything baby, mommy and daddy. These could be signed out by the receptionist, just the way we borrowed books in elementary school before computers obliterated the ritual of signing them out, thus depriving a generation of children their weekly occasion to invent adult, rococo signatures. This was not an office, not a clinic, but a cozy, charming storefront boutique. It was like hot soup or a favourite sweater. This was a place where moms were made, not patients or diagnoses.

It matters. For what it's worth, I have my blind guy's take on the significance of these design issues. Our senses condition us in these situations. The purpose here was comfort and care, and all my senses were combing the room for those effects, reading into the environment, looking for signs. Nothing communicates the alienation of the medical establishment better than recycled air, sharp fluorescent lighting, discarded magazines and the ubiquitous hiccups of electronic noise. But none of that was present. Our senses were calmed and appreciated. That's a helluva first impression. What matched that attention was the length of our visits with Andrea and the team. Each one lasted about forty-five minutes. Most doctors, of course, are hard pressed to exceed seven. In Andrea's office we lounged on more comfy sofas and overstuffed chairs and jawed about babies, about every detail of how Tracy was feeling, or I was feeling, or about how the poem "Which One of You Built the Bomb?" actually went. Whatever we needed.

"Let's maybe talk a bit about how you guys want to see the labour," Andrea began.

"Fast is good," Tracy suggested.

"And painless," I added.

How peculiar, to recognize Andrea's voice as she talked with Tracy about our preferences for the delivery. I was in home room in high school again, only this voice from my past was advising my wife about our future. No awkwardness infected the dynamic, either. My relationship with her had been so long ago, so short and so teenaged. Tracy couldn't have cared less. But what did occur to me, as Andrea put her hands on Tracy's growing belly, is that the world gets smaller as we get older.

Over the next few months we would build a plan of where and how we wanted to have the baby. Hospital or home, our choice. Hospital, please. Who wants to say, "Whew! Now that we have the baby, let's mop the floors and put on some laundry!" Seriously, though, should anything go wrong, both Tracy and I wanted the security of a hospital and all its expertise and equipment right outside our door. Andrea also asked us what tests we would like to have, or not. Would you care to sample an ultrasound? Why, yes, thank you. Our choice. Would you like the triple serum screening done for Down's syndrome? Sure, since you asked so nicely. The centre of gravity, the control, was given to us.

"Would you like to hear the baby's heartbeat?" Andrea asked at the end of our first meeting.

Of course she would have done this anyway, but everything was phrased to us as our choice. Maybe in a few months

I'd hear, "Would you like to boil some water?" I'd put the kettle on, as if we were about to have tea. Such politeness really moves me.

Andrea got out the Doppler and turned on her midwife's stereo. Tracy lifted her shirt and lay back on the couch to let Andrea search for a signal. I could barely stand listening to the expanding, crippling silence as she searched and searched for the baby's heartbeat. Nothing emerged but static and the rhythm of Tracy's own thump, thump. I began to sweat.

Andrea angled again. Still nothing. Another angle, another nothing. I could hear my own heart growing louder in my ears. A person can have a heart attack listening to these things.

Then she found it. The pattern was faint and fast, like rabbit punches. Something small scurried between the surefooted steps of Tracy's heart. Andrea found an angle to bring those traces into the foreground. The baby's heart sounded to me like the pictures I remember of a sun coming out from behind an eclipse, a searing edge that eventually engulfed the frame in white light. There it was, brought to the foreground. A new heart. No photos, no ultrasounds, no lesser experience for me. Here I was on equal footing, and tethered by my ear to fatherhood. My mouth smiled big and stupid. I felt finished with an unnamed terror. A worry that I might not have the feeling of fatherhood in me when I heard the first expression of my child.

The baby's rhythm, in a funny way, found me. Like a little cane, it had tapped out my own echo-location, and let me hear a bit of myself as a dad. Just a bit. Then Andrea turned the machine off, and the baby disappeared back into Tracy, distant and dark again. Fatherhood, during pregnancy, ebbs in and out of men this way. Strong, then light. Concrete, then abstract.

Before we left, Andrea asked if we wanted to learn the sex of the baby after our next ultrasound. Had we considered the issue yet? Discussed it? We hadn't, so for the next week or so, I turned the idea over and over, studying the differences I could imagine, or not imagine, between a boy and a girl, and what it would mean to know which way we were going.

Though I grew up in a room stuffed with brothers, oddly enough I found myself unsettled at the prospect of a boy. I thought back to the games and toys of my youth—the skateboards, the pellet guns, dismembered He-Man action figures, everything that my brothers and I had bent into the service of our experimental cruelties. Snails and magnifying glasses. Rocks and cow shit. Big rocks. Then bigger rocks. As I tried to imagine myself about to step outside and play with my son, I thought about the games my brothers and I had asked of our father. I remembered standing in the street with him throwing a baseball back and forth. An unparalleled treat. His pitch was so fast. A cannonball that arrived in my glove, and a sting that electrified my arm. I'd wanted to throw like that. A father didn't make an effort. He was a force, that thing behind a hammer, a car, a baseball. A capability of hands to lift you up to the first branch, where those same hands let you loose to climb.

Thing was, of all the stuff I recalled my father doing for me, and the stuff I used to do with my brothers, none of it seemed within my capability any more, not as a blind man. Imaginative play as I'd known it as a boy had left with my sight, alienating me from what had once been a natural instinct. I couldn't imagine what I would replace my old play with, or how. I would have to learn to play all over again.

I'm not saying that what we did as boys was strictly visual. But maybe our play was less inclined to the pleasures of narrative. Hit something. Throw something. Ride something. Do something to something. That's a boy for you. But as a blind guy, my sense of fun had transformed with my body. Now I was about words and stories. These I can use to navigate. These I can manipulate. In these I can play. Pretend.

Maybe a girl would propose something completely different. Girls were, after all, a mystery to me. How do they play? I thought about tea parties. I could play that. Dolls. I could make up dialogue. I could dress a Barbie, I guess. The job is tactile enough, although I'm not strong on colour coordination. My daughter and I could play house, I knew how that went. Hell, I could be the blind father in that game and spill pretend stuff in the kitchen. Or for real drama, I could pretend to wound my pretend son with a pretend baseball, and then get into a pretend car accident as I pretended to drive him to the pretend hospital, where my daughter would pretend to be a doctor, and pretend to save me from my pretend collapsed lung.

But how girls play was simply speculation. When we were kids my sister was off doing her own thing. I was so much older than her that we might as well have lived in different countries. I needed to know more. So one night when we were sitting at my kitchen table, sharing some sushi, I asked my sister what she actually did when we were kids. Her answer was revealing.

"One of my favourite games," she said, "was coma."

"Coma?"

Erin had never struck me as a Goth sort of girl. She was very matter-of-fact about it. Nostalgic, even.

"Yeah. Oh, coma," she swooned, as if repeating the name of a fond, forgotten boyfriend.

Her pause, or reverie about her childhood game, continued. Maybe she was just busy chewing. Or perhaps she was playing coma.

"And? So, like, you just lay there, playing like you were just, uh, lying there?"

"No," she said. "I pretended I was in a coma and that I was just waking up. You know, for the first time in years."

"And then what?"

"Then I'd do it again."

My sister, it turned out, was way more interesting than either of my brothers had ever been.

"I also collected cigarette butts in a baggie," she added. "Sometimes I would pretend to smoke them, but mostly I just collected them."

Why hadn't I thought of that? I can remember staring at our empty cul-de-sac, certain there was nothing to do on it, or to it. But there must have been hundreds of butts I could have collected. Erin and I could have traded. We could have started a store, got the other kids hooked, and grown our own neighbourhood black market.

Erin's list of games expanded in scope and complexity. For a time she'd enjoyed affixing paper clips to her teeth as braces, and for a spell she'd written regularly to the public transportation authority to collect their used bus stop posters—her prized score was a wall-sized cartoon of Burt Reynolds and Loni Anderson playing *Win, Lose or Draw.* One year the only toy Erin had wanted was a cash register—a real one, thank you—which could then be mysteriously robbed as she lingered in a coma, or could be used to sort the money after cigarette butt sales. At school, dressed in her best clothes, she told teachers and friends how busy she was, what with her grandparents visiting from Ireland, having left their castle just to see her.

Meanwhile my brothers and I had just punched things.

Maybe Erin wasn't like every girl, but if my daughter had any of our blood in her, I wanted to play. I could start combing the sidewalks for cigarette butts immediately and have a decent collection by our due date.

I grew more and more attached to the idea of knowing the sex of the baby. Some parents make the practical arguments for early disclosure—you know what sort of clothes to buy, what colours you might paint the room. Names. All that jazz. But something else ultimately made the case for me, something small and concise.

In imagining the play of boys and girls, I liked having a pronoun. He or she. No more, "the baby," or, ick, "it." Nicknames made the whole thing feel even more fictional. While Tracy's bond was already physically growing through pregnancy itself—the intimate disorientation of being one person with two hearts, for instance—I couldn't help feeling somewhat left out. All dads report this, sure. We feel suspended in pregnancy's abstraction. That's why we always want to feel the baby kick. We crave descriptions and reports.

In a way, it felt as if there was another home inside our home, but I was looking in on it from the outside, and I wanted to be closer. No, Jesus, nothing Freud would tug his beard about, but I craved something like giving the baby a hug, the way all people want to be as close as possible to the things they love, and to thereby hold and know the shape of them. The language of "he" and "she" offered an approximation of that warmth. The certainty of "he" or "she" would hold the baby for me, give it shape. My picture and story would be more focused for it, more animated by the precision of a word. More real. Why not sooner rather than later?

Before I could float any of this by Tracy, Andrea called. Two weeks had passed since our last appointment. She had some test results. We had math to consider. Math, after all, is the primary language of an unborn child. All they can tell you is what you can measure. I hate math.

"The test for Down's syndrome," Andrea said, "came back positive."

The initial shock of that phrase, and its punch, made me doubt the clarity of its meaning. Positive, she'd said. That's a good thing. She meant the good positive, right?

"Positive," she explained, "doesn't mean the baby necessarily has Down's syndrome. The triple serum test has a lot of false positives. A lot. What it means for sure is that your test results showed a one in two hundred chance that the baby has Down's, and we consider that at the very edge of the positive range."

I thought about the likelihood of what we were discussing. A half a percent chance of something happening. That seemed to me to be about as un-positive as you could get. But the only way we could know for sure, we learned, was through amniocentesis, which involves extracting amniotic fluid by poking a needle into the uterus. Amnio itself has risks, though. A one in two hundred chance of inducing early labour, and that is precisely the math used to determine if a triple serum test is positive. If Down's is more likely than, or as likely, as inducing early labour—a risk taken to absolutely determine the baby's medical status—then it is considered a positive test result.

Can I make alien calculus clearer? I doubt it. I felt like I was getting a crash course in accounting methodologies from Enron's chief financial officer. This was not the simple path of pregnancy that I'd grown up with, and been taught to fear. When I was a teenager it seemed like a girl could be living on Slurpees and Ex-Lax and happen to kiss somebody. Next thing you knew the baby would drop on the arcade floor. Presto.

"What you need to decide," Andrea advised, "is if this is something you want to know for certain, and if the risks of amnio are worth that certainty. A one in two hundred chance isn't a great risk, but given other markers on the ultrasound—which could in themselves indicate nothing—I would say your chances are more like one in a hundred."

Just like that, our chances doubled. Lightning would cook me any second now.

"But it's up to you guys," our midwife added, as midwives do. "It is still very early in the pregnancy and you have every option."

Tracy was stunned. Like me, she raced to process the math, trying to navigate how likely our chances actually felt, and what action they asked for. The ratio of one to a hundred didn't feel like anything in and of itself.

"What would you recommend?" Tracy asked Andrea. "I mean, if it was you, what would you do?"

"It's really your choice and what you feel most comfortable with. The risks of amnio and the likelihood of Down's are pretty much equal."

On occasion, a case can be made for the benefits of giving over control to others. Sometimes it's nice to defer to their wisdom and experience, and to escape the responsibility of hard calls. This was one of those moments. It felt natural. I wanted somebody to guide us.

"But what would you do?" I asked again. "You, Andrea, not you, the midwife?"

"I don't know. I'm not you guys," she said.

It was true. We were not the typical family, if there is such a thing, and Andrea seemed aware of the conversation we needed to have, but had yet to discover for ourselves. Tracy and I both tried to imagine life with a child with Down's, which for us meant a life with yet another disability in the house. How I would play with my kid was the furthest concern now. Without having to say much, Tracy and I both understood that the workings of our lives would grow incredibly complicated. The gap between our abilities as parents would grow even larger, and Tracy would be weighed down with the task of holding three diverse bodies and their idiosyncratic needs in concert.

Math is a funny thing. A one percent chance, a concept without an image. As we mulled over our options, both of us drew and redrew pictures in our minds of what that concept looked like. We were talking about picking one penny in a pocketful of change. That didn't seem so bad, or so likely. I was teaching four classes at the time. It would be like running into one of my students at the grocery store but trying to guess who it would be. No way. I can't even remember all their names. If somebody told me I had a one in a hundred chance of not making it across our street, I'd still cross. All the good shops are on the other side. The real chances of me surviving traffic with a white cane are probably worse than that, and yet I still leave my house. What were we worried about?

But then picture this: if somebody said you had a one in a hundred chance of winning the lottery, you'd probably call yourself lucky.

The meaning didn't come from percentage itself, but from the pictures in which we dressed the numbers. Math didn't help us see.

I finally gathered the courage to ask Tracy what she needed. To risk early labour with amnio? What if it was positively positive?

"I think," she said, "if we had the baby, and then found out we should have done the amnio . . ."

She trailed off, testing her conviction one last time. In her mind she saw pictures of another life. Pretend.

"I don't want it to be this way," she said, "but I think things would get so hard, and I would have to make up for so much that you can't do, that I would resent you and it would eventually end our marriage."

That was it. She could see what the numbers described.

She was lying on the couch staring at the TV. The show *Rock Star* was on, so I knew she wasn't watching. Tommy Lee was about to announce who would become the next most rockin' rock star of rock.

"It would just be unfair for all of us," she finished.

The story was painful and true. We could say things like, "We shall overcome," or I could get out my guitar and sing "All You Need Is Love." We could chew the scenery about how it didn't matter whether the baby had Down's or not, we'd remain a family, dammit, and push on—insert Disney soundtrack here. But sentimentality is not a helpful form of pretend.

Tracy had played out a version of our lives with brutal honesty, which is what the math needed. A story. Now we knew what we had to do, and why, though we felt no relief in deciding to risk early labour. We just had to know.

I stretched out on the couch with Tracy, our baby, and its chances, and listened to the TV. *Rock Star*'s winner was announced. The audience screamed. I imagine miniskirts flying. Men pumping fists in the air and shrieking like babies. Rejoice, they told us. Somebody beat the odds. Somebody is the chosen one.

Needling

• • •

We readied ourselves to go to the hospital. We would have our amnio test today. It had been two weeks since we'd learned of our Down's chances. For us, a visit to the hospital was becoming commonplace, like a trip to Home Depot. We were well practised at the ultrasound routine, and between two pregnancies Tracy's uterus had become better photo-documented than, say, my face.

But this trip got off to a rocky start. I was lacing my shoes, a pair Tracy had given me as a birthday present, when they reminded me that Tracy and I share a birthday. Same year as well. What were the chances? I pictured the calendar, and all the possible years of months and days we could have divvied up as distinct birthdays. Then, as I tied my laces, Down's seemed as inevitable as a Monday.

Meanwhile, Tracy struggled privately with the unknowns of amniocentesis—the significant pain of the needle, the long wait that would follow, and the risks involved. In life it's always better to be early than late, but, of course, not until you arrive in the world on time first.

We left the house in a fluster, and ran into our neighbour Steve and his young son, Max, who were playing at the bottom of our stoop by the fence. Or on the fence, then under it, and repeating the pattern as necessary.

Steve and Max were part of a recent surge in our neighbourhood. Around the time we became pregnant, every new family in town moved here, or every new family in our neighbourhood had been, until now, stowing their infants in cupboards. Most noticeable were the expanding brigades of fancy strollers, like bitty tanks with equally bitty soldiers inside, that ambushed me as I caned along the sidewalk, feeling for safe passage. Then again, because of our pregnancy, I also had to wonder if I was simply experiencing an old visual phenomenon—you know, the certainty that if you get a Day-Glo orange Honda, forty cars just like it will be parked on your street the next morning, and then you'll need sunglasses just to fetch the mail.

Steve and his wife, Tat, had bought their place in our complex maybe two weeks after we'd bought ours. I remember watching—well, sort of—from the window when they moved in. The sidewalk was busy with the smeared shapes that belong to people, and these shapes ran up and down the stairs carrying the kind of blurry objects I've come to recognize only as blurry objects.

I called to Tracy and said, "Hey, toots"—to have used her real name would have signalled a serious query, if not danger to my person—"I think we've got new neighbours."

She looked out the window, but rather than enjoying the people and blurry objects, she seemed concerned. She makes a funny noise when she's troubled, something like a small, defeated grunt. It's cute, but worrisome at the same time. She had good reason to worry, too. Steve was unloading swords.

Now, here's a hard fact that will remain true of this world: swords do not have many positive applications. I would encourage my child to stay away from them, or anybody who happens to be holding one. Another hard fact is that rules have exceptions. Steve and Tat, for instance, turned out to be exceptions to my sword rule. Their weapons were just decorative, maybe some sort of family heirloom. To date I've never once seen Steve in the courtyard doing Jedi impressions, polishing his armor, or practising Middle English. He is, in short, neither an eccentric medieval hit man nor a budding samurai. We've never mentioned the swords.

But Tracy's troubled expression was about more than Steve's swords. His wife, Tat, hurried back and forth between the moving van and their new house, probably eight months pregnant. For a moment, Tracy saw her own ghost.

I finally met Steve because the phone company wired our number to his house. He kept getting calls for some guy named Ryan, so out of curiosity he called his own number, and I answered. We became friends after that, sharing drinks and stories on the stoop while Max crawled about, grew, eventually stood up, and now experimented with the physics of our fence.

We were running late for our hospital appointment. Tracy unlocked the car as I listened to Max play. I imagined him playing with my son or my daughter one day, though I had a filing cabinet of objections ready if my daughter should be courted in the future by an older man, and one with family swords at that.

Before I got in the car I mentioned to Steve how fast his little blur moved, and Steve noted that since Max had taken to solo-powered adventures, he'd discovered four favourite new activities: running back and forth, swinging on the gate (who can blame him?), climbing the bottom two stairs, and banging a stick. That is, banging a stick while he walked. Like me.

"Don't ask me why," Steve said, "but he seems to think the way you go is, well, the way to go."

Max scuttled by my little tunnel vision and I heard the banging noise of his stick. He was playing blind man. From all the giggles, I'd wager he was having a pretty damned good time of it, too. More than I've had.

And that's when it really hit me: what if my son needs a stick? What if my daughter picks up a stick one day, just like her Papa, out of curiosity, or adventure, or fun, or admiration. But what if she picks it up and doesn't get to put it down? Max gets to. He dropped his stick and returned to the grand mystery of swinging on the gate. But how would my kid be able to do that if one hand had to cling to a stick?

I know what you're thinking. It's hard to believe that I'd never considered the effect of passing blindness to my own child. If I had, it had squatted in the back of my mind as a vague concern at best. I knew that there was a very small chance of the baby manifesting my condition, which was also contingent on a billion factors to do with Tracy's genetics. A very small chance. But with all the other threats and troubles we'd experienced, I'd never really looked any further into it. Now as the baby grew more and more real every day, I could feel myself on the precipice of guilt. My knowledge of my own condition was limited. I'd never secured us any hard reassurance that, as I heard it from my doctor so many years ago, I am an idiosyncratic case. Spontaneous.

The chances of my child going blind were there, but negligible. I think.

Even more peculiar was the fact that Tracy hadn't asked. Maybe because she fell in love with a blind man, she felt she couldn't turn heel on the idea of having a blind child. His blind child. Ours. Why hadn't we talked about this before? Hard to believe it had gone unspoken, but it had. The spouses of the blind are a mysterious people. In some ways, it would appear, they are more accepting of blindness than we, the blind, are.

I let the thought go down. It was too hard to look at, too piercing. Besides, I told myself, the idea of my child being blind didn't have anything to do with love. Blindness couldn't make me want to have a child any less. Could it? Should it have?

I didn't share any of these thoughts with Tracy. She had enough to worry about this morning. At Women's Hospital they were planning to push a fat, hollow needle into her belly, and they were hoping to stop just shy of the baby. They would have the baby's picture on a screen and would use it for guidance. But I had to wonder. If I'd allowed the picture—of a child with a stick—to stay in my head, if I'd let that image into my mind's eye more often over the past few years, would that have guided me to do anything differently?

Just to think, before the baby had even arrived in this world, it was already surrounded by the threat of swords and sticks and needles. No wonder babies come out kicking.

Tracy and I drove to the hospital and didn't talk much. As she fought with traffic and honked the horn, I felt a familiar uselessness. Simply put, Tracy was driving herself to the hospital for a procedure. There she'd suffer the pain and anxiety of amnio, and afterwards, although sore and perhaps dizzy, she'd drive herself home. My contribution?

"Want the radio on?"

"Doesn't matter."

I turned it on and fiddled until the volume was just right. Then I went back to being inert.

My hand scratched my chest absent-mindedly. I noticed the texture of my T-shirt's print. Suddenly I felt underdressed for the occasion, and not just underdressed in a minor way, but in a manner that could invite all the bad news a hospital can muster, all on account of inattentiveness to my appearance. Because we were en route to the one test that could definitively reveal what was going on with our baby's development, it seemed wrong to have worn a T-shirt that read "George Bush and the Gang: The Fucking-the-World Tour." Blind people forget they project images, and that those images mean things to other people.

What if the hospital employees disagreed with the sentiment? What if the fates disagreed with my politics, too? And what should one wear to an amniocentesis test? Normally I would give more attention to gum stuck under my chair than fashion, but I was immediately overcome with a feeling, a suspicion, that we were not only going for a medical exam, but applying for the baby's health. Like a job interview.

The baby would come to know this magical thinking in its life. When we have no control, we invent mechanisms. Rituals and superstitions and games to ease our helplessness, or compound our fear. As a father, I would hope to teach my child not to believe such superstitions, and not to step on cracks in the sidewalk.

Tracy turned off the radio.

"Hey, I could've done that for you," I said.

"It's a button."

"I'm just saying."

We arrived at Women's Hospital right on time. Inside we were greeted by a pungent blast of air. Or something like air. Hospitals smell unhealthy. Perhaps it's because medical institutions actually smell of human beings turned inside out. Hard to say. That or the industrial-scale production of cheese omelets.

Our first stop was upstairs to meet with a genetic counsellor. Despite the name, a genetic counsellor is not necessarily someone who is inherently predisposed to helping others, although that may be the case. Rather, she was another well-intentioned professional who would steer our fragile psyches around the rocks of a particular niche market: couples trying to foresee the future. Psychology is often as interested in creating a particular mind as it is in treating it.

Our counsellor was a pleasant and rumpled woman who ushered us to seats at a small, round table in her office. She hauled out a number of pens and pads of paper, and for a moment the scene intimated that we were about to make crafts at the Busy Table.

"I'd like to begin," she said, "by sketching out both of your family histories. We'll make a family tree for the two of you."

So we were, indeed, going to make crafts. In this particular drawing, however, the trees would represent a chronology of marriages, and the fruits of those trees would be the various illnesses and genetic misfortunes those marriages had brought to bear. A happy tree. The tree of life. The view from high up in its limbs shows you just how weak and fucked-up you really are. Then your children fall out of it.

"Let's see," she continued. A pencil scratched broad strokes on a piece of paper. "Ryan, do you have any history in your family with any specific illnesses?"

My instinct was to lie. I had practice. Back when I took tests to map the deterioration of my sight, the doctor would place my head in a machine where lights would go off like small fireworks. In my hand was a joystick, and I was told to press the button when, or if, I saw any mammoth, intense spotlights, or even faint blips. I didn't see squat.

I did, however, hear the machine belch and pop, noises that I assumed were followed by lights. The darkness was too much. I could hear my blindness the longer I sat there. So I lied on the test. I listened and pressed the button occasionally after the machine made one of its burping sounds. I wanted to pass, even just a little, even at the expense of what I was there to learn.

I felt the same when asked if my family history had any causes for worry. Fudge the edges, keep hope alive. The counsellor waited, pencil poised.

"Oh, not really," I said. "A bit, I guess. There's maybe some mental, uh, stuff. Illness—bipolarity. Clinical depression. Just a bit."

She and her pencil waited some more. I stared at the smear of my feet, not looking up at my family tree and its fruit.

"And where in the family?" she prompted.

"Oh, you know, mostly just my brother, for sure."

My younger brother Rory had suffered harsh and chronic depression, and had died of an accidental drug overdose when he was twenty-two. I'd written about it, but didn't care to tell his story again just now. The counsellor could know about the depression, but she didn't need to know about its outcome, I figured.

"Do you have other siblings?

"Two. They're fine. Another brother and a sister."

Hopefully Erin's paper clips on her teeth weren't clinically motivated.

"And is there anybody else in the family with bipolarity or depression?" the counsellor asked.

"Not really. My grandmother, I mean. My mom's mom."

The pencil sketched a new branch and some more fruit.

"And a cousin," I added. "Or two."

"On your mother's side still?"

"And an uncle."

Her hand picked up speed.

"And how about your father's side?" she asked.

"My father? Well, my dad isn't technically my biological dad. Might as well be, though."

"Okay. Tell me what you know of your biological father's side."

My mother remarried when I was three, having divorced my biological father after I was born. That's basically where his presence, and my knowledge of him, ended. My interest, too. Why seek out unnecessary ghosts? Ma was a woman who kept the past behind her, and I had to respect that. I don't need to open doors to ask why they're closed.

"All I know's his name," I said, "but sometimes I'm not sure if I made it up."

"Anything else?"

"Nope."

I withheld my suspicion that he was an asshole. Didn't need to add that to the gene pool.

By the time we'd finished mapping mental illness between both families, our tree had a lot of fruit, the weight enough to crush our baby, and we hadn't even begun to map the cancer or Parkinson's or Lou Gehrig's disease or—

"And what about your sight," the counsellor asked, "is it a genetic condition?'

The threat of Max and his stick resurfaced.

"Uh, yes. I have retinitis pigmentosa. There's no family history, though. I'm a spontaneous, uh, mutation."

Mutation had even been the medical term used by a retina specialist when I was first diagnosed. I'm a sporadic morph. Ryan, the man from mutation. Secretly I've always liked that part of my blindness. It always seemed more punk to be a biological deviant than to have, say, slipped in the tub and banged my head. Nerdy.

The counsellor continued her questions with renewed excitement. RP was genetic, and she was a genetic counsellor.

"Do you know much about the transfer of RP?" she said.

She sketched out the basics. My condition is matrilineal, carried on the X chromosome. For women, one X chromosome with bad information can be augmented by the other. That's how they can be carriers of my disease without manifesting symptoms. With only one X, however, a boy's chances are greater, making it more likely that little Billy Blindo will join me on the bus.

"I'm guessing that you have concerns about your child inheriting the condition," the counsellor said.

Before I could answer, before I could apologize for not having considered this earlier and not having made it a central part of my planned parenthood, Tracy answered for us.

"We're not that worried about it."

The counsellor was stunned. Me, too. "Are you sure?" she said.

Tracy deferred to me. "Are you concerned about it?"

"Sorry, but it hadn't crossed my mind much. Probably should have, but it didn't. I guess I just pushed it aside in all this."

Tracy brought the focus back to the issue of Down's, and since there was no family history, the counsellor said she really couldn't help us foresee the chances any better. At least our crowded tree, as far as we knew, didn't have Down's along with everything else. That was a good thing. In the end I was glad I couldn't see our final tree. A lot of pencil lead was used.

"I'll call you," she concluded, "when the amnio results are in. Should take about two weeks."

Before we left for the procedure, I had one question.

"When you call," I said, "can you just say what the results are, so I don't think I know by your tone of voice? You know, or by something else you say, like, 'How are you?' or whatever?"

"How about I just say hi and that the baby is fine?"

"Or hi baby's fine."

"Gotcha."

"Thanks," I said. "Or, if it's, you know—"

"I know."

She promised to be blunt and fast. A practised killer, or saviour.

Tracy and I navigated our way back downstairs, through the halls to the ultrasound clinic. Along the way I picked up wisps of grief, medical terms I couldn't understand, requests for paperwork, discussions about surgery and "options." Wheelchairs rolled by and I caught the occasional sound of IV stands dragging behind shuffling slippers. Hospitals are as much a rhetoric as a place. The mere fact we are in one suggests, without kid gloves, that everything is wrong. Everything.

A bubbly young clerk took Tracy's information, shackled her with a hospital bracelet and sent us to the waiting room to do just as the room demanded. Tracy picked up a magazine and aggressively flipped the pages. The only other time she does that is when the plane is taking off or we've hit a patch of turbulence.

For a moment I considered a latte from the kiosk behind us, but the idea of taking a coffee break seemed about as appropriate as my T-shirt. The only other option was brooding, so I really put my shoulder to it. I gathered the day's details in my head, the image of a little kid with a cane and Down's, the hospital smell, Tracy's soft belly, the divining needle and the low whispers of passing doctors. All of it constellated, then bloomed into a plain but potent thought, one I could quietly pluck and offer to my gal as conversation.

"Trace?"

"Yeah?"

"I feel like a gorilla," I said. "I think you may have married a gorilla, genetically speaking."

"A gorilla?"

"Yeah. Sorry about that."

Tracy continued to flip through pictures of what I assume were smiling, computer enhanced stick-women.

"Well, I'm a pincushion," she answered.

Her tone was dull and resigned. The way a talking pincushion might sound. I grunted in agreement, her gorilla mate.

"So," I said, "you're really not worried about RP and the baby?"

"Of course I don't wish for it, no. But when the counsellor asked, she might as well have asked if I was worried the baby might be normal, or might take after you."

"I thought that was just me."

"I'm used to blindness, too, you know. It's about as normal in our house as air."

We left conversation at that. We were simply waiting now, and we would be waiting after the test, too. We were among these people now, the couples knitting and crosswording and sipping coffee in chairs next to us. The waiters.

When our time came, the bubbly clerk ushered us into a small debriefing room. A woman, a nurse with a perfect French accent, greeted us. Hers was the first reassuring sound I'd heard all day. I felt the edge of hope. Only good can come of anything said in a French accent. Paris is our favourite city, the rich food, men in scarves, wine with lunch, a city of bon vivants and existential crises.

This nurse, Our Lady of Hope, went through some paperwork with us, highlighting important facts and information, then showed us where to sign. Tracy put my hand on each spot and placed the pen just so, then I let my signature rip. The last time we did this, we bought a townhouse.

"I must inform you of zee reesks of amnio," the nurse said, "but zay are very small. About one perzent of zee prozedurez can induze la-bur."

She smiled. At least it sounded as if she smiled, the kind that negates what was just said.

"But az I zay, it eez a very, very zmall reezk. Very zmall. Trauma to zee baby from the needle eez also a very zmall reezk. Very zmall. You muzt be aware before we prozeed."

I didn't feel comforted any more. Perhaps no parent wants

to know that there is any risk whatsoever, or to be told that they are knowingly putting their child at risk, even though parents do it all the time. Pavement is a risk. I remember going over my handlebars at the age of seven and planting my face on the street. Supper is a risk. I remember choking on a hot dog. My father grabbed me by the feet, hoisted me up by my ankles, like a fish strung by its tale in a trophy photo, then he whacked me on the back until a bit of Oscar Meyer bulleted from my mouth.

In the room where they perform the procedure, Tracy and I were greeted by the attending physician, Dr. Tessier, and her two assisting nurses. They reassured Tracy that the procedure would be quick and that many women report the pain is little more than a pinch. Tracy handed her coat to one of the nurses and dropped her purse on the floor beside my chair. I sat in it facing what I thought was the screen, but would later learn was just a wall.

Tracy lay back on the bed and they gooped up her belly. When the image came up on the screen, the doctor and her nurses conferred.

"The baby is sitting quite high," the doctor said, "so we can't approach from the preferred angle."

She said it as if I knew which angle that was, or as if Tracy did. What was to be preferred about it? A moment later I knew she wasn't talking to us.

"You could come in this way from the right," the ultrasound technician said.

"No, the doctor said, "I think from below is better."

"The placenta is obscuring some visibility, so maybe here would be best. Coming this way."

All the talk of "this way" and "here" and "there" gave me no picture. The staff sounded like professional curlers on the ice debating the best approach for their next rock.

All the while our baby was there on the screen, just an idea of colours in my mind, and slowly growing in the dark. I wanted to warn the baby about the needle. I wanted to tell the baby about swords and sticks and good people.

Finally the doctor said, "We're going to insert the needle just below your belly button, Tracy. The needle will go through the abdominal wall, so you'll feel a little pinch, okay? Okay, here we go. And, there. And pressing now—"

My body throbbed with adrenaline and sympathy. I needed to do something, to help Tracy somehow, to let her know that she wasn't on her own, though in the most critical sense she was. So I sprang to it, damn the consequences, to take back some control of our lives and hopes.

I grabbed her purse from the floor, and sat back down.

"Keep still," the doctor said to Tracy.

I dropped the purse on my lap. A man of action. Her belongings were safe from these, these—helpful professionals.

"There," the doctor said, "we're through, all done. Just keep your feet up for the rest of the day and don't do anything stressful, okay?"

I bet Tracy had a thought, something like, "You mean like going for another amnio?"

• • •

We had two weeks to kill. They nearly killed us. Every time the phone rang I had a heart attack. Then the two weeks tipped into a third and we both imagined the causes of the delay. Nothing obvious came to mind, such as a busy queue of tests, or an understaffed summer shift at the lab. For us, a third week meant that the results were bad, and the staff was double-checking before giving our genetic counsellor the nod to do her best flat delivery of blunt force trauma.

It was late afternoon when the phone rang. If it was them, why were they calling so late in the day, I wondered. Had they been putting it off? Had the counsellor been practising her delivery? I hoped it wasn't her. The timing was awful.

"Oh, I need to speak to—is this Ryan?" she said when I answered.

The bad news was all over her voice.

"Yes?"

"The baby's fine."

I told Tracy, who was standing beside me in the kitchen.

"Thank you," I said. "That was very well put. Thank you."

"Well, I practise," the counsellor said. "Now, do you want to know the baby's sex? I have that information, if you'd like it."

We did want to know. We'd decided it would be our treat, if the baby was healthy, if it was okay.

"She's just fine," said the counsellor.

Our Unmentionables

• • •

As the baby grew in Tracy's belly, a staggering protectiveness, and paranoia, grew in me. My awareness of our constant proximity to one catastrophe or another became acute. The power of my mind's primal state was fed by poor weather, too.

An Australian once told me that Vancouverites sound like "British surfers." If not an accurate description of our speech, it is a true characterization of our weather—rainy, tepid days for beach bunnies in mackintosh jackets. Once in a while the rain freezes, however, and entombs the city in an icy shell. That was what happened the morning of our first prenatal gathering.

Our destination confused me. I assumed we were heading to a gymnasium infested with yoga mats, upon which we'd spend the day breathing and watching films about drugs and hot towels. Stuff like that. Prenatal class stuff.

Instead a seven-months-pregnant Tracy and I hauled pillows and brown bag lunches to our instructor's house. I don't recall the brochure specifying that the day's events would unfold in her basement, but there you go. Still a better arrangement than a warehouse prenatal franchise, if there is such a thing, which if not, I'm sure Wal-Mart will be offering in Aisle 6 any day now.

We skidded into a parking spot. The ice then threatened to take Tracy down as she stepped out of the car. The threat mounted further as we skated around to the trunk and retrieved our pillows—or safety cushions, as I began to think of them. Getting nervous? I was, and because Tracy's belly already made it difficult enough to balance, I insisted on steadying her elbow as she walked, to ensure her safety. A gentleman, and a scholar. And, er, a blind man guiding his pregnant wife through the Arctic.

How're them nerves doing now?

Tracy felt similarly.

My death grip served us fine, until my feet shot out from under me and I spazzed across the street, doing the funky chicken, yarding Tracy along and, yes, practically slam-dunking her face into the concrete.

In the end she was the one who kept us upright. Maybe the baby was enough to counterbalance my, you know, help.

The point is, from this I derived my first prenatal lesson: don't help unless you're sure you're being helpful. With that in mind I carried on.

"You go first," I insisted as we reached the stairs.

They were steep and old, crumbling concrete that rose from the sidewalk, through a yard and up to a rickety house swelling with the unborn. Tracy planted a foot on the bottom step and began climbing.

"You go first," I repeated, for no apparent reason.

"I am, I am. Just gimme a sec. Jeez."

"Take your time, and I'll follow," I added, displaying my facility with the obvious.

As she hoisted herself up each step, my pillow secretly followed her in the catch position. One good sign was the lack of any broken, pregnant bodies piled at the bottom of the stairs.

The day's soundtrack greeted us as the instructor opened her front door. The noise didn't come from her fuzzy television—it wasn't that sort of soundtrack. Rather, I heard yelping. A shrill percussion of tormented babies? Tiny, tiny mothers in need of epidurals?

"Oh," the instructor chuckled, "don't mind the noise. I breed pocket dogs. I've got a new litter. C'mon in and take off your shoes."

She was a doula to all species. Later, straddling an exercise ball, she would instructively gyrate and wail—you know, to horrify us with how guttural things were going to get during labour—until her new pups joined in. Birthing doo-wop with pets.

The other couples were already gathered in the rumpus room, as if waiting for a slumber party. Tracy guided me into the middle, around murmuring voices and their feet, where we sat on the floor, all ten chairs having been taken. Tufts of dog fur stuck to my palms as I lowered myself to the carpet. Or basement-sized hair shirt. There was some worried talk about the snow outside. I heard men authoritatively refer to salt. Other conversations criss-crossed the room.

"I've read that in some cultures," one woman said, "they eat the placenta afterwards. Isn't that interesting?"

"Really?" another voice said. "I guess that must be in places where there's a lack of food or something. God, I don't think I could do that, no matter what."

I repressed my natural impulse to say, "Excuse me, but if you're not going to eat your placenta, can I have it?"

"I've also read," the afterbirth fetishist continued, "that some consider the placenta to be the baby's twin and so they leave it attached until the baby decides when it wants to separate."

"That's beautiful," another voice said. "Isn't that beautiful?"

She must have had a unique eye for interior design. Keeping the placenta for company? I tried to imagine the logistics of such beauty. Do they make maternity sweaters with a placenta pocket? Maybe I would be charged with carrying the placenta around in the Baby Bjorn until, I don't know, until our daughter was old enough to say, "Would you get that thing out of here? It stinks!"

"I've read," a man said, "that some people plant it under a tree. Continue the life cycle. We like that idea."

Though the instructor was busy setting up her videos and sorting through her notes, she chimed in.

"I had a client last week who did that. It was a wonderful home birth. He played his guitar the whole time, which helped keep us moving until it was the baby's moment."

I began to feel unprepared. Or maybe under-ritualized. I assumed we needed to glean technical know-how here. Science. Information by the binderful. Charts and hospital processes. Categories of anaesthesia. It had never occurred to me that the contemporary birth asked for so much customization and performance. Others in our class had already scripted entire theatrical experiences, having even chosen music, and specific aromas to waft through the hospital air, to be among the first sensations given to their newborns. Then out would come the placenta sweaters.

"I feel sort of bad. Do you think we should do something like that?" I whispered to Tracy. "Something, I dunno, showy?"

"Like what?"

"I dunno. Like maybe I could—"

"You're not playing your guitar."

"But do you want to pick some music or something?"

"You're not playing your guitar."

"I could bring the stereo."

"I just want to keep things simple," Tracy said.

Elegant simplicity has always been her style. She picked some dog hair off the back of my shirt.

"Whatever you like. Simple is good," I said. "I mean, not that I wouldn't have practised up and stuff. But I'll be too busy, anyway."

Doing what, I didn't know. Hopefully by day's end I would have a clearer picture.

The instructor signalled to us that she was ready. We were curious how the class would begin. We'd heard stories. According to some friends, their prenatal lessons kicked off with a shock-and-awe style of learning. Their instructor initiated the class with a clip from the film *Crouching Tiger, Hidden Dragon,* specifically the scene in which the heroine takes up her machine gun and lays waste to a bar full of men.

"This is how women feel during labour," the instructor highlighted for our friends.

The lesson couldn't have been more plain, or more tailored to life in the southern United States. When preparing your hospital bag, do not pack the family M-16 with the baby seat and high-protein muffins.

But that's not how we began.

Now, maybe it's a side effect of my blindness, but I collect phrases I'm dead certain I'll never hear again, the same way sighted folks archive photographs of novel visual moments. My favourite phrase so far—and pregnancy is a bountiful source of previously unheard phrases, let me tell you—was the first question our prenatal instructor put to me.

"How thick are you?" she asked.

And so we began. I stood in a row of skittish men who, along with our seated audience of wives and girlfriends, waited for an answer. Nobody offered one for me. Of course I couldn't eyeball a guess, so I measured my thickness with a pinch of my finger and thumb.

"Well, oh, I'd say I'm a good half-inch."

"That's right!" the instructor chirped.

She seemed pleased with my hands-on ingenuity.

"And how big is your hole?" she asked.

Another gift—that made two collectible phrases before noon. They were coming like buckshot.

I poked a finger into my hole. "About an inch, I'd guess."

The role I was asked to play in our birthing class called for more than method acting. No emotional memory could help—I was a cervix.

Role-playing seems to have permeated every arena of instruction. You can't walk through the park without dodging the corporate executives falling from trees—a public peril of trust exercises—nor can you rest comfortably on a couch without a therapist imitating your difficult mother. It's a wonder folks have any time left to act like themselves.

Such pedagogy is ubiquitous enough that, well before Tracy and I arrived, I already knew that the day would demand some participation from all the soon-to-be fathers and labour buddies. Gone are the wallflower privileges of direct, bone-dry information and, thankfully, gone are the days when fathers-to-be were expected to bring little more than cigars to the maternity ward.

Problem is, now we don't know what to do.

Not that I was alone, as cervixes really are. The five other men in the class played the same role. We stood shoulder to shoulder, each of us representing another stage in labour. A cervix gallery.

Our prenatal instructor turned her attention to the rest of the class, explaining that I was at the early stages of effacement. I had a long way to go until I would be supple enough for the baby to pass. The dinky plastic donut in my hand—intended to further illustrate my dilation—felt heavy and perfect, like a knucklebone our pug, Cairo, would enjoy chewing.

Unfortunately, our stage play wasn't dramatizing the plot fast enough. The cervix next to me had a question. He'd asked it twice already.

"And so now do we drive to the hospital, or what?" he said. "I mean, I just want to know exactly when we need to go, that's all."

I didn't know his name, but Tracy had quietly described a few classmates to me as we'd lounged in the dog hair and waited for our instructor to begin, or to finish delivering a puppy. I knew this fellow only as the man whose T-shirt shouted, "Canada: it's F-ing Cold here!" His question about departure time seemed similarly nuts-and-bolts, if not equally alarmed.

"Please, just relax. Labour partners always want to know when it's time to go," the instructor said.

"We sure do," said Mr. F-ing Cold.

A number of men mumbled their agreement. I imagined some were poised with personal scheduling devices, ready to jot down their hospital ETAs.

"Trust me," the instructor said, "your wife will know when she wants to go. She'll definitely know."

Some of the women chuckled knowingly. We, the men, did not.

"And, so, would that be, like, around now?" Mr. F-ing Cold asked. "Even roughly speaking?"

"Well, just look how small Ryan's opening is," the instructor said, slightly exasperated. "There's no urgency. He's still got a long way to go before his baby can pass."

I held up my hole, remembering that I was a visual aid and should act as such, and showed it around the way school teachers display picture books. Tracy and I were seven months pregnant. In the name of education and our unborn daughter, I was going to be the best damned cervix I could be.

Not that my participation came easy. Tracy and I aren't into interactive fun. We're the ones who pop Ativan when actors break through the fourth wall. But, faced with childbirth, rising to the occasion is what nature demands. For any partner standing beside a pregnant beloved, the prenatal class marks our own passage into a funhouse of identity. Here we can admit that we are uncertain of our interim position, the one that begins with contractions and ends when we pay the hospital's parking lot attendant. In between we're uncertain what to do, what is to be asked of us and, most important, we're motivated by these feelings to selflessly invent a few irrational expectations of our own.

The language of pregnancy was telling me as much. At seven months I should have recognized that given Tracy's growing belly and the associated discomforts she had been dealing with, any indulgence in the fantasy that "we're" pregnant was bygone. A dangerous sentiment to toss about, too. I was simply orbiting now, ready to lend whatever I could to what would soon become a primarily one-woman show, and to try to keep her from feeling alone in it. The other five men knew the same, and were equally perplexed about how to go about living up to their own standards of limitless support and dedication.

As informative cervixes, we at least got in touch with just how in need of something to do the non-pregnant labour partners really are.

But if I thought being a cervix was a tough immersion, what followed snack break asked even more, possibly too much.

We made a "sharing circle."

The first task was to sit around and admit what relaxes us. I'm still surprised Tracy didn't go into labour right then just to dodge the sharing part—I would have—but, let's face it, discussing the calming effects of *CSI* reruns seemed a better introduction to labour than, say, five men doing placenta puppet shows.

What the husbands feared most about birth soon came up. Mr. F-ing Cold was up first.

"Hospitals," he said. He didn't miss a beat. "I'll be fine before we arrive, and I'll be fine when we leave."

His wife sighed.

As he prattled on and made his wife feel more and more alone, it became clear that this was a helluva tricky question. The men had already been warned that the focus must always be on our partners, not on ourselves. No doubt. All things considered, we'd nothing to grouse about. Consequently, the best fear one could admit to, and with honesty, was something that offered the most support to our partners. It's like writing on a job application that your main weaknesses are perfectionism and a penchant for working late.

"And what would you say your deepest fear is?" the instructor asked the next guy.

He hemmed and hawed for a moment, then phrased his answer as a question, testing its effect. I think he was an engineer.

"Uh, I'm afraid of the pain?" he asked.

The room listened. No heckling, so he carried on.

"I think I'm afraid of the pain my wife will experience?"

The room murmured warm, reassuring tones. His confidence returned.

"Yes, I'm afraid for her pain, and I just don't want to see her have to go through it," he finished.

Some were on the brink of applause.

Like a perfect Olympic dismount, he added, "But whatever she needs, I'll be there."

He was pure gold dressed in angel's wings.

"And it's not about me," he added.

Mr. F-ing Cold shifted in his seat. His wife sighed again.

"All very common feelings," the instructor said. Her voice was soothing. "Very honest. Good for you."

I could tell, however, that the other men in the room seethed with a different judgment. He'd beat the rest of us to the right answer, the good and perfect one. Now it ceased to be good and perfect, and just became used.

Nobody doubted his honesty, of course. His fear for his partner was all too real, as was all of ours. But it also seems to be a genetic defect that men thrown together are incapable of interacting without imposing competition on the situation. Even if it is about honesty, eventually we'll make it competitive honesty.

A series of small, piercing yelps echoed from upstairs. Everybody froze and, I imagined, looked at the ceiling.

"Oh, the puppies," the instructor swooned. "They're biting each other a lot the past few days." She turned to the next couple. "And tell us about your fear?"

The man opposite me shifted in his seat and muttered a bit, looking for the rabbit in his hat.

"I think if I'm really honest with myself, I think I'm afraid for the baby. That it will be . . ."

He trailed off into soul-searching, and we hung on the drama of his line. Either that or he was gauging our reaction, to check that he hadn't said the wrong thing so far.

"Yes, I'm afraid," he finally determined, "and I'm afraid that—and I don't mean this in a bad way—but I think that, in all honesty, I'm afraid that the baby will be, I mean, what if it's ugly."

He seemed proud of his finding. Perhaps he forgot, however, that sometimes naked honesty can feel an awful lot like the wrong thing to say. He finished his insight.

"All I'm saying is that I wonder if a parent can even see that their child is funny looking. Know what I mean? What if the baby doesn't look as beautiful as I hoped?"

The room went to dead air. Then our instructor, remembering her job, muttered something supportive and encouraging, the way all teachers do, despite the impulses to reinstate corporal punishment.

"Good for you. Honest. Very honest."

And it was charming. Sort of. Mr. Ugly Baby let it all hang out with such innocence and sincerity, the way I imagine my little girl will, one day, present me with a gift of dandelion stems and a selection of dog poop. Her collection of miracles. And who's to say they aren't?

Mr. Ugly Baby would get his soon enough, anyway. He became our instructor's foil during the sideshow admission of her own fears. She began by holding up a bottle, displaying it to everybody but me.

"Let me show you one of my fears. What's this?" she asked Mr. Ugly Baby.

He ventured an observation. "Baby oil?"

"Wrong!" the instructor shouted.

"Looks like baby oil to me," said Mr. F-ing Cold.

Maybe he just wanted somebody to kill him.

"No! This baby oil, ladies and gentleman, is garbage! Toxic garbage!!" the instructor said. "And what should you do with it?"

"Uh, you spread it on the baby?" said Mr. F-ing Cold.

The instructor slam-dunked the bottle into a wastebasket she'd planted nearby.

"That's what you do with garbage!"

The room returned to dead air, except for the dogs who were busy eating each other upstairs.

The instructor composed herself and explained her little bit of theatre.

"My fear is this: your children will see you drink from water bottles. What do you think they will do when they see this bottle? They'll think, oh, how lovely—water. Then your child will pop the lid and . . ."

Tracy didn't need to explain. The instructor mimed a child glugging something down, using the same motion that suggests somebody is a drunk. Maybe the kid with a taste for baby oil is comparable or something.

The rule in our instructor's house, we were told, was that if you can't put it in your mouth and swallow it, then it can't go on your skin, either. Where this left soap, I don't know. Sweaters and T-shirts, too.

Despite my best efforts, I didn't escape the scrutiny of the sharing circle. Eventually I was called upon to confess my fears. I did my best, but I have to admit that I plucked a thought that came almost too easily.

"I'm afraid my blindness will get in the way when Tracy needs me most."

The world was warm tones and reassuring murmurs. People seemed genuinely impressed by my insight and honesty, and were happy for Tracy. Myself, I felt like I'd just tried to surprise them by declaring fire is hot. Wasn't my fear obvious? Hadn't they seen the pregnant woman helping *me* cross the room?

While my fear was real, it wasn't the whole truth. For now, however, there was no good reason to attach words to the things unsaid between Tracy and me. It didn't feel right to share, in front of strangers, emotions that we hadn't expressed to each other on our own. The unnamable, sometimes, is just that, and is best left unnamable.

None of this is to diminish or to detract from what the women here were about to go through. Not at all. This is just to observe that the majority of fears felt by the men in the room were simply unnamable. That's what frightens most—the unknown, the unimaginable. We were all preparing for that, and no sharing or role play could help us conjure the words that belonged to that unknown. Whether they were words describing the fears and joys headed our way, or helping us hang on to our partners during labour. Something was coming. Something mythical was on the horizon. That was all. The only thing I knew was that I needed to make room. Even just a little. That meant getting my own shit out of the way, not talking about it.

Pain management was the final lesson of the day. We were asked to arrange ourselves in an imitation of various complex positions our instructor adopted. We had knees bent, chairs turned upside down, and pressures applied from a number of angles. I thought of flesh and origami. I tried to keep up, but it was like being asked to assemble an IKEA bookshelf while somebody read me the instructions. No pictures, just point A goes into slot C and rotates with pin W, and so on.

When the instructor checked our progress, Tracy was balanced on her hands and knees, and I was crushing her hips with my forearms, or something.

"Like this?" I said.

"No," the instructor said. "Turn around. No, this way. Now do this."

"Do what?"

She did something.

"This," she clarified.

"What do you mean by this? Like what? How? Like that?"

She grabbed my hands and bent them around Tracy's pelvis, bringing my arms parallel to her thighs. I'd been very,

very far from doing that. Tracy was already sore from my delivery of pain management.

"Now do I push like this?" I said.

The instructor seemed exasperated.

"No," she said, "push on Tracy this way, like this, and down, and up, and down."

"I don't see what you're doing."

Tracy got up. "I'll just show him later. Go ahead, we'll just watch for now."

"But I'd really like you to—"

The instructor said something or other about the importance of practising, but Tracy and I both knew, without a word, that we were acquiring more problems than solutions. While the instructor had the best of intentions, and couldn't have known otherwise, she was giving Tracy more to do. No way, during labour, could Tracy steer me with the specificity I needed, no matter how well-intentioned our teacher was, or how much I'd shared about my fears of blindness getting in the way.

Blindness just does.

Tracy knew it, and I knew it, as only we could. So, we were perfectly honest and opted out of the model of labour support that has become the convention. Instead of trying to give Tracy whatever she needed, I would give her what I could.

Shortly after that, Tracy and I found ourselves knee to knee, each squeezing an ice cube in our left hands. We were told to sit in silence until the cold melted away. Then, taking up fresh ice, we were asked to squeeze again and, this time, to talk to each other. The purpose was to experience for ourselves how words help diminish pain. Silence, the reasoning goes, amplifies our ache.

"I'm sorry," I muttered, "but I don't know what to say. I just don't know what I can say to help you through this stuff."

"I like that," she said.

We sat quietly, and melted the ice with our hands. The quiet was clear and articulate, and rich with the kind of understanding only couples can know after many years together. It was our privacy, and our greatest comfort. Both of us knew, without a word, that we wouldn't come back the next day. We would find our own way to do things, as we always do, and always have.

Before we left we watched a video about birth positions. The picture went fuzzy on occasion, but the instructor's rubber hammer pulled it back into focus after a few whacks on the TV. Didn't matter to me. The narrator did a fine job describing what none of us could see, especially during the climax of labour.

"Now," he said, "arch your back like a rainbow."

Only Tracy laughed out loud. She knew what I was thinking. A totally collectible phrase. She still uses it to correct my posture.

Feel Anything?

• • •

The phone wouldn't stop ringing. I couldn't stop taking my frustration out on the person at the other end of the line.

"Is this Mr. Kingston?"

"God, no."

"I'm sorry. I mean Knight. I'm calling for Brian Knight."

"That's me."

"Hi, Brian! I'm calling on behalf of—"

"Great, you woke the baby."

"Excuse me?"

"The phone. It woke her. She, her, is a baby, who is awake."

I'd pace about the kitchen a bit, sounding frantic, perhaps readying a bottle. Or gathering the minor kitchen implements necessary to murder a telemarketer.

"This will only take a minute, Mr. Kinsman, if—"

"Look, I'm trying to put a baby to sleep here—and it's hard, you know."

"I, uh . . . would there be a better time to call?"

I liked, "When the baby is grown," but usually I hung up.

A little venting felt top shelf. Instructive, too. Blindness has immeasurable power. It can excuse me from all sorts of stuff—designated driver duty, plenty of jaywalking, impossible queues at airports and banks—but, wow, a newborn was a step up. What righteousness a baby confers upon a parent. What unassailable virtue.

And I wasn't even a dad yet.

Our daughter was due at the end of January, and as Tracy's due date approached, things started to get a bit strange around the house. Well, I got a bit strange. It didn't help that people were calling every ten minutes to ask if the baby was here yet, or, as they put it, "Well? Well?" Telemarketers were only one of my releases. For another I would punch my talking clock, causing it to shout the hour in self-defence. No exaggeration, I believed that I could make the baby come if I made it well known how late she was. I also checked the calendar on my laptop several times a day to urge things along. This is as ineffective as rapid-firing the walk signal button at an intersection, but I also did that whenever possible. Maybe the sense of urgency would reverberate all the way to Tracy's uterus.

A mom has every reason to want things to get under way. Tracy announced several times a day that she was done with pregnancy, thank you. She felt tired and massive. My hurry simply stemmed from a need to know everything was okay in there. Come out and show me. Come out and need me.

After the due date passed, I found leaving the house just too exhilarating, and too disappointing, to bother. I could go to the gym, say, where I could kill a decent couple of hours, but my sense of imminent crisis would tag along for some exercise of its own. Once, in mid-curl, I even caught myself heeding the lyrics to Amy Grant's "Baby, Baby." How could I not? They pulsed from the PA system like bullets into my skull. If the sappy, empty sentiment wasn't bad enough, the baby-fixated hook, which repeats "baby, baby" until it hurts—as hooks in your ear tend to do—convinced me that Tracy was at that moment doubled over in contractions, unable to call, unable to move, without any hands ready to catch the—sing it with me—baby, baby.

I couldn't run home fast enough. People talk about the eerie powers of intuition and divination that come with an imminent birth. Labour had begun. I knew it. I burst through the front door and heard an unmistakable sound.

Tracy was eating a sandwich. Upright. No paralysis, or emerging infant's head accompanied her lunch.

Rationally speaking, I'd learned in our prenatal class that contractions and dilation take a long, long time. We could expect hours before they reached a point where the word hospital should even be spoken.

But that was months ago, and probably a lie, and, really, I just didn't want to fuck up before we even started.

So I opted to stick around the house, in case. Tracy would put it another way. She might tell you that I opted to annoy her with conversation-starters such as, "Feel anything?" or "So, like, how are you, uh, feeling?" Expectant father warning: I highly recommend you fly the above questions off the nearest dock. Your tongue will go missing if you don't.

This isn't to say Tracy was a model of Zen calm, though. She was certainly tapping her watch and practising her own magical thinking. She was just better at hiding it. An awful lot of pages were turned after the due date. See what I mean? She burned through a crazy number of books. It was all about starting new chapters. I was on to her.

Another day passed, then another.

My mind often migrated into the future. I spent much of the day inside little fantasies of our family life to come. These imaginings were exceptionally detailed, and kept me distracted enough not to make the waiting any worse.

For instance, one morning I trudged up the stairs and paused, listening to the incessant earworm in my head. I imagined that it, the song "Baby, Baby," was actually blaring from my daughter's room. Then I imagined how I'd tell her to turn it down, and I scripted how the two of us would have an elaborate father–daughter standoff about her stereo. Can't say I liked her attitude much. Still, some turns of phrase showed her facility with appositive clauses, which she knows damned well are my favourite grammatical structure. The kid knows how to play me. What can a father do? Then I imagined her best friend—no, the other one, the *best* best friend, who was also hanging out in the room, and I imagined how she would titter as I left, and how she would tell my daughter that her dad is weird, the way he stares at your earlobe when he lectures you.

Then I'd surface and try to recall what the hell I came upstairs for.

Hours, it seemed, were spent inside such vignettes. The stories warmed me, just as my imagination had warmed me on Christmas Eve when I was a kid. Back then, like most sentient beings, I would lie awake conjuring all my possible gifts, and play with each of them in my mind until it was time to get up. Sometimes it seemed so much better, all that potential, than the limited finality of whatever I was about to find under the tree. Possibility is such a pleasure and thrill, with its many lives lived at once. Now, before the baby had even arrived, I'd lived with a teenaged girl who left popcorn on the couch, and I'd enjoyed days with a toddler in her little pink skull-and-crossbones toque who chased the dog about the kitchen, shouting, "Mine poopy! Mine poopy dog!"

Another day passed, then another.

By February, and well beyond our due date, I had composed a list of banal but pressing last-minute questions. A moment at the living-room window, feeling the winter sun on my face as I stared at the blurry speck of lawn in front of our house, prompted the most serious of them all. I turned to Tracy in a panic, stung by my lack of foresight.

"Where the hell is she going to play!"

I didn't add a question mark. Tracy looked up from the pile of receiving blankets she was refolding for the tenth time.

"Play?"

"That's not a yard," I explained, "and the street is too busy. Where will she, like, go?"

Growing up on a suburban cul-de-sac, I spent most of my childhood in the middle of the street, or on our sprawling front lawn. Cars drove around us. Lawn mowers, too. What deprivation was I about to impose on my unborn child? What sort of spatial poverty was this?

"Kids find places to play," Tracy said. "I'm not worried about it."

She went back to her blankets.

But the lack of lawn was my first failure to provide. It stuck with me. It stuck in my craw even though my siblings and I had found much pleasure stuffing ourselves under the kitchen sink. I sought other advice. I confessed my worry to my friend Jim, who also happens to be a blind writer. If anybody would sympathize, it would be Jim. He understands me.

"Don't worry," Jim said, "kids always find somewhere to play."

Liar. Besides, what did he know? Jim entertained neighbourhood kids by deploying an empty stapler into his forehead. What did he know about play space, other than it could be found above his eyebrows.

Nothing quelled all my bubbling, trivial concerns, or my new behavioural tics, not until I realized the real problem, or at least the real cause of the vignette making, the punching of the clock, the baiting of telemarketers, and my budding yard envy.

I was nesting.

We'd readied things, bought a crib, a car seat, diapers, the whole range of normal preparation and impulse. Regular, generic-brand nesting. But now I experienced another dimension of the phenomenon. High-end nesting. An incredible mental frenzy. I fretted about everything that was beyond my control, which is all you can do after you've painted the nursery, arranged soothers, and filled the freezer with tuna casseroles. Nesting is also about tidying the fringes of duty and promise. So this is what nesting really feels like, I thought. It was sort of similar to meeting a celebrity. A celebrity emotion.

After a few days of this, a whole new feeling visited me. I woke up one morning purged and spent. Totally. I felt done, as if the big day wasn't approaching any more. Waiting for the birth wasn't like Christmas Eve any more, or even New Year's Eve, but more like January eighth. A flatness settled into my bones, the kind that dogs you when the festive season is over. Back to business. The baby hadn't come, so, clearly, she wouldn't. I'd outwaited her, in effect. Ah, well. Say, do we have any postage stamps around here? What should we have for supper?

Tracy, of course, felt otherwise. She wanted the baby out. Preferably before our daughter could say hi. In the meantime Tracy's mom, Helen, had arrived to stay with us. Helen is, like my own, the Platonic ideal of a mother—cheerful, organized, calm, capable. A woman who can pickle beets while doing taxes. She waited patiently, reassuring us that things would happen when they needed to happen, which was not entirely self-evident to me. Helen just went about her day, modelling her own patience, often at the kitchen table sewing towels, or knitting by a reading lamp. I thought of a mythical Fate weaving my future. How nice to make your own towels. And destiny.

Waiting be damned, I mustered one last push for influence, and took Tracy to see *Borat.* Maybe if she laughed enough, that would jostle things up a bit, or make the baby want to come and see what all the racket's about.

Borat, I discovered, does not induce labour.

Another day passed, and another.

I woke up on February sixth to find Tracy pacing the living room in pain. Not the kind that passes under the surface, never registering its jolt on your face, but that outwardly ouch-ouch kind of pain. She even made a few noises I'd never heard from her before. Slightly drawn-out moans, sometimes similar to those adopted by bad actors who want to portray indigestion. But really, really terrifying.

I dropped all preoccupations. Time to get to work. Then, as if by reflex, I became Mr. F-ing Cold from our prenatal class.

"Let's go to the hospital. I'll get the bags, and your mom can drive," I said.

Tracy sat on the couch and moaned, then stopped. Somebody had flicked off a switch. I half-imagined the baby cackling like a mad scientist, wringing her hands over the power button to her new torture device. I rephrased my plan.

"Ready to go when you are," I said, quoting the gospel of Mr. F-ing Cold.

"No, it's fine," she said. "The contractions started about three o'clock this morning."

I couldn't believe it. I'd slept through the first five hours. Now I really needed to do something to redeem my participation.

"I'll call Andrea, then."

"I don't think you need to do that. The contractions are still far enough apart."

How could she be so sure? We'd just driven off a cliff and she was telling me we still had time to check the brake fluid.

Tracy reminded me to time the contractions and the duration in between. Of course I was supposed to do that. We'd discussed it when I was a cervix. Tracy's mom pulled out her knitting needles and resumed her post, wise to what lay ahead, having seen this movie twice before. Having starred in it, I mean. We waited for the next contraction. Ages passed.

"Here comes ano—" Tracy said, and got up to pace the hallway as the contraction bit off the end of her sentence.

I nailed my eyes to my oversized watch, ready to log and track. I angled the face, got up and angled it another way. Tracy tried to pace by several times while I contorted and searched for enough light to focus my tiny window of clarity. The light was too poor in the living room. For years I'd been too vain to buy a watch that could talk. Now I was without the only tool I needed to do my only job. My big talking clock was upstairs, so I abandoned technology altogether. I had a backup plan.

"One Mississippi, two Mississippi," I began. Thirty more followed.

When the contraction finished, I started over again. Yes, aloud. The next contraction wouldn't arrive for half an hour. That's a lot of Mississippis, and a lot of extra pain to inflict.

My tally didn't get very high before Tracy took my watch and gave my job to her mom.

No problem, I thought, I'll supervise. My ears listened to Helen minding the watch. We were a team, kind of. She was the driver, and I was the broken headlight.

Tracy spent the day in a rhythm of couch, contraction, pace, then repeat as necessary. Helen knitted, while I fetched food or pumped up the exercise ball for Tracy to sit on, or rolled it from room to room to change the view, not that she looked at anything, what with her eyes closed or fixed on the floor as she groaned and worried a path back and forth.

From that moment on, the experience of labour was entirely hers to know, and mine only to observe. Of that I can say this much. Those early hours are a strange threshold. Much in the acoustics astonished me. I could hear that we were in a liminal, fluid time, of contractions increasing in frequency and duration, thereby accelerating Tracy's routine. As the pain elongated, the pauses shortened. Each shift in measure intimated the approach of the baby, as if something, some force, were circling, closing in tighter, and tighter, each time it cycled around. Or maybe it was spreading, spiralling out of Tracy, a widening gyre, and filling her voice, my ears, our house with a more consistent, more intense, and, my God, more audible presence. Say what you will about the spectacle of labour, but the sound is something else. A storm approaches likewise. A rumble is at first separated from the lightning, from the event, but the calm between shortens as the storm closes in on your little place in the world. Eventually the sound and the fury are on top of each other, a blinding clap thunders overhead, and it's here, with you, or for you, in a flash. Tracy's quickening moans became more like cries, then calls. A beacon to guide our daughter home. These cries were not Tracy's either, but distinctly other, as if channelled. By ear alone I would not have recognized her as my wife. Whatever the reality and its secret description, this much I knew for sure: I heard an oncoming baby, which, for a time, was all that could be done. Nothing to see here, not yet.

Tracy said she'd tell me when to call the midwives. I kept my shoes on. Because I could do little more, I also readied her bag, and even lined her shoes at the door. I couldn't wait. Soon we would deliver Tracy to somebody who could actually do something on my behalf. To understand that last phrase is the kicker. To get a professional involved is the core, or so I suspect, of men's fretfulness about getting to the emergency room zippity-pronto. We imagine, even subconsciously, that the doctor or nurse or midwife is truly an extension of our role in the birth. They are the hands for our useless hands, bystanders like us, but with know-how, and we want to get to them so we don't fail.

At some point during the pacing, and now the occasional bath, Tracy's mom had turned on the TV. She watched *Oprah* with one eye while she knitted, or helped Tracy in and out of the tub, or cheered her on. Helen's was a reassuring presence. She knew what Tracy needed, which I didn't, and knew when it was needed, which I didn't, not unless I was told. But language had begun to fail. Tracy's words were colonized by moans. I could no longer rely on her to illuminate things with their names. Without words I was cut adrift even further.

But Helen carried on where my blindness left off, and she kept the house feeling normal. I was so grateful, and jealous. A part of me was still a child who wanted to say he could do it all himself, though he couldn't and he knew it. None of this was about me or my independence as a disabled guy, and so my usual determination had to go. Strange to think of that as the contribution I could make. Be less independent, in order to help Tracy.

Then I heard something else. Not Tracy's escalating, guttural cry, but Oprah's guest on the TV. Something in me sparked. An irrational anger, a rage. The celebrity actor wanked on about the big jet he'd parked in his big driveway, and about his philanthropy and how good it made him feel. He seemed to be overwhelmed by, if not suffering, a big-ass case of self-congratulatory, warm, fuzzy feelings. It irritated me much more than it should have.

"Would you turn that off?" I snapped at Helen.

My tone caught me off guard. It was without gratitude, and unnecessarily biting, as if the TV itself had slapped me. Helen turned the tube off cheerfully, although a bit taken aback, I'm sure.

The anger was specific. This was it, this was labour, this was the day my daughter would meet me. What would I recall? Lots. And some celebrity's big, stupid jet in his big, stupid driveway. That was wrong. I didn't want him or Oprah or anybody else intruding on the most important day I would know. No trespassers allowed. Not in this, my memory. How does one protect it?

I was busy peeing in the corners of my mind, as it were, when Tracy puked and asked me to phone the midwives. One of the team, Amy, answered. She told us that Andrea was off for the night. Amy would be with us instead. Fine with us, we loved them all the same. A saviour's a saviour.

While I was on the phone, Tracy marched her eighth mile back and forth, her voice locked in a protracted wail. You had to wonder where the air came from. A note held as even and taut as a tightrope, long as a freeway.

"I'd say she sounds just shy of five centimetres," Amy said, "but I'll come and check. You probably have a couple of hours to go before you need to head to the hospital."

Those are ears to envy. I've come across comparable sensitivity before, but only in blind folks. Once I met a blind guy who could click his tongue and hear by echo-location how far away he stood from a window, or if the window was a wall, and if the wall had a door he could walk through without so much as a bump. That was nothing, though. You should have seen him select a sandwich at the buffet table. Or consider Joybubbles, the infamous blind hacker who, back in the 1950s, could whistle the precise frequency of the old dial phones, and thereby dial around the world for free. To my list I had to add Amy now. She was like a concert pianist, a woman whose ear was so tuned to the music of her art that she could measure dilation by phone. For that she deserved an honorary white cane.

And she was right. Within two hours we were in the car and driving to the hospital, Helen behind the wheel. She dropped us at the emergency room doors and sped away to park. The safety of modern science lay before us in all its underfunded, bureaucratic glory. I ran ahead of Tracy—perhaps for the first time in our marriage—found the doors, and held them open. And there I waited.

And I waited some more.

"Trace?"

Nothing.

Maybe she'd gone through another entrance? Was this an entrance? A body blew past and thanked me. How progressive—hospitals hiring blind doormen. Finally I went in search of my wife, who until a few minutes before could have been heard for a good city block.

I caned back along the sidewalk until I found Tracy hanging over a handrail, hurling her guts into the bushes. We'd made it about four minutes shy of a perfect arrival.

Here's proof that unconditional love exists in this world. Tracy, now in second-stage labour, slowly guided me down the hospital corridors, skirting me around gurneys and wheelchairs, until she found the elevator, and then, despite a contraction, ushered me in and among the crowds of sickly and well. Hers is a monumental strength and selflessness. She could have been one of those pioneering women who skinned caribou and felled trees until their water broke. She could easily have abandoned me to a security guard for safekeeping, or left me to catch up with her at my own pace. But she didn't.

Though I didn't know it at the time, in the elevator I stood too close to the person in front of me. Worse, because I was facing the wrong way, I also inadvertently pinned my eyes to that person's chin. No escape for them.

My sweaty hand clung to Tracy's elbow, as Tracy continued to pace on the spot. Her breath was laboured. I cheered her on, repeating, "You're doing great, babe, doing great." Some in our elevator may have misunderstood. I was, of course, referring to the labour, not her ability to park me as close to a chin as the owner's sense of chin-privacy would allow.

It's called a hospital, or a ward, but these did not describe our destination. We congregated with Amy and Helen in what felt to me like a pretty decent hotel room. Tracy didn't opt for the usual tour, though. She didn't test the mattress, or see what was in the closet. Instead she immediately grabbed the foot of the bed and shook it. Violently. She generated an earthquake. As it radiated down her arms she seemed determined to drive the bed frame through the wall and into the next room. She would've, too, if not for the woman in the opposing room doing the same thing back in our direction.

No longer could I recognize Tracy's voice, nor could I keep up. She stripped down, was in and out of the birthing tub, several times in fact, but always she returned for a spell to the foot of the bed, and braced herself against it like a pinball wizard. The damned thing just wouldn't go through the wall. In a movie she might have simply reposed on the mattress and panted a little, maybe grunted twice, and that would have been that. The baby would have gently slid into the world, as if ejected from a revolving door at Bloomingdale's. That cinematic moment would have been my cue to beam proudly under my surgical cap. But where was my surgical cap? Hollywood has this whole thing so wrongheaded. Perhaps nobody within the studio system has ever been present for real labour, or given birth, or been born themselves.

"You're doing great, Tracy. It's very common to go through this standing up," Amy said. "Just do whatever your body wants."

Tracy didn't have any plans to do anything otherwise, until finally she spoke.

"My hips," she cried. "Do something! My hips are going to break."

That was the signal. A clear one. Amy and Helen went into action. Hot water ran in the sink. They cooked up a soup of towels. The famous hot towels had arrived, and so had the boiling water. So this is what they're for, I thought, though I still didn't know what they were for.

"Here," Amy said, and handed over two towels. "Put these over her hips and massage them. It'll help a lot."

Another familiar voice chimed in, uninvited.

"Yes, it really feels so good to help people," Oprah agreed.

In my mind she mumbled something about angels and hope.

Tracy's hips seemed to be on the move again, along with her voice, so I readied myself. My hands held the towel open to net her on a pass. When her moan returned to the foot of the bed, I pounced. Sort of. I stood there and considered pouncing.

"Go on," Amy said. "Put the towel on her hips and—"

But I was afraid to touch her. Though she was about to pass a planet through a straw, for some reason I worried that

I might hurt her. Break her or something. She was in so much pain, too much to possibly bear the weight of damp cotton.

"Where are her hips?" I asked.

"Here," Amy said, and guided my hand towards Tracy. "Come closer, this way."

I shimmied cautiously. Tracy urged me to hurry.

"Here," Amy nudged me further. "No, here. No, closer."

"I just love to help," Oprah swooned. "Don't you?"

I brought my towel in for a landing, and along with it I unknowingly brought all my weight down on Tracy's bare foot. Boot heel to bones.

Tracy screamed with a new voice. In prenatal class we were told to listen carefully. I acknowledged the new scream and massaged her hips more vigorously. Meanwhile I ground her foot into powder.

"If we work together," Oprah cheered, "we are the angels!"

"My," Tracy cried, "foot."

Foot? Labour really does involve the whole body. Before I could massage her foot, Helen pulled me back. Then I realized what I'd done. Tracy whimpered and tried to walk it off.

What else could I do? I dropped the towel and recoiled. Amy reassured me Tracy was fine, and nudged me back to carry on. But I handed my other towel to Helen, who took it and stepped in for me. Helen stayed that way, on my behalf. Tracy and her hips were happier for it. Knowing my limitations has always been as important as exceeding them. Yes, it felt good to help. Help by getting out of the way.

Tracy and I had agreed we'd find our own way to do this. We did. After I crushed her foot, I took a post better suited to the way in which my body could complement her needs. I crouched down beside her ear. I would be her focus and her distraction, which is what I've always wanted to be, to some degree. My jabbering presence talked her through the contractions, said to push or not to push, whatever message Amy asked me to deliver. This I could do. I was the pony express rider. The town crier. A guide, for once.

"Okay," Amy finally said, "just one more, Tracy, one more big one. Ryan, do you want to catch the baby?"

Catch? That's not a question frequently put to a blind guy. When was the last time I caught anything other than a cold? But maybe I could do this. The idea of my hands being the first things our daughter touched in this world was an overwhelming thought. And after all this labour and pain, it also seemed unjust. Tracy's should be the first.

"Do you?" Amy pressed. "Quick."

"No," I said.

That choice would be the template of many to come. The real question was not whether I wanted to catch the baby, but if I felt I could be responsible enough for her to take a chance, to gamble my ability against her well-being. I didn't feel ready to risk it. Not yet.

Just after one o'clock in the morning, four hours after we'd arrived at the hospital, and after one final, crippling push, Amy caught our daughter for me, and put her on Tracy's chest to warm.

"Hi, Tess," Tracy said.

I crouched down beside the new voice, and reached out until I touched Tess's arm.

"Hi, little mouse," I said.

I squinted hard. So hard. In the speck of clarity in my right eye, I caught what looked like dark hair, then it disappeared and became a colour. Round colour. An eye. A greenish eye, perhaps. Less than half of it appeared to me. Just an edge of the iris and the tip of its outer corner and lashes. The eye blinked. Because I couldn't see anything else, I wasn't sure if I was staring into Tracy's eye, or Tess's. It seemed like a colour and curve I once knew. I repeated my hello.

"She's looking at you," Helen said.

Tess recognized my sound, and turned to it. Already a little like her papa. We are guided by voices.

ACT TWO

• • •

Unrest

Sootherface

• • •

Everything has its blind spots. Even a perfectly good eyeball has one where the optic nerve connects to the retina. Parenting has too many blind spots to count. They multiply by the hour, and define one's peculiar dance as a father or mother. After all, parenting is often little more than a set of flailing reactions, typically when it's too late, say, as a little hand discovers how car keys slide nicely into the one wall socket you didn't mortar behind bricks. In other words, you don't choose what you get right, only what you get wrong. Thing is, that's part of the fun. As long as it doesn't involve voltage.

Of all the blind spots we've encountered as parents, I can safely say that the greatest, at least so far, was the week after Tess's birth. From the moment we exited the hospital, and maybe for longer than a week, we had to ask each other: *What the hell is going on, what are we doing, what are we supposed to be doing, and where did you put the brochure about this?* I mean, heaps of videos and books and classes and consultants devote their attention to pregnancy and the art of labour, and enough breastfeeding information is out there to fill Alexandria, but nobody said boo about life immediately after the hospital parking lot. Not even a fortune cookie on the subject.

As we climbed into the car, it occurred to me how surreal our brief time in the hospital had been. We'd glimpsed the rock star life. We'd blown into town, made peculiar demands—would you spread a rubber tarp over this floor?—basically trashed the hotel room, then left the hired hands to mop up the bodily fluids. It felt oddly criminal. We'd gotten away with something. A heist, of sorts.

"Just think about it," I said to Tracy as I buckled my seat belt. "I need a licence to go fishing, but we can just leave with a baby."

Tracy and her mom tried to connect straps around the baby. Another blind spot. We hadn't practised securing the car seat, which was about as user-friendly as a particle accelerator.

"And isn't it weird," I continued, "to think that we arrived as two, and now we're leaving as three. We've multiplied. Or is it subdivided?"

My curiosity was my own. All Tracy wanted to do was go home, have a small, stiff drink, and reacquaint herself with our bed. Preferably without any need to pitch it about like an empty pizza box. But as Tess cried all the way home, only then did it occur to us that, oh yeah, sleep or any other frivolous item on the agenda was to be scheduled by Tess now, not us. Babies are basically autocrats.

Blind spots, like black holes, have a gravitational pull. The same physics applies to a wailing infant's mouth. Tess cried and cried. It engulfed my ear, and drew me to her every gasp, yarding my head around from the front seat to stare and fret. Compulsive, but incredibly useless. No matter. This was my new mind. From now on she would swallow most of my consciousness. At that I felt a new terror, and a new wonder.

Our home, its routines that fortify my sanity and reinforce my character, changed the moment we walked through the front door. You can't help but encounter your material world for the first time. Even the most trivial thing takes on a charge of genuine alien invention—the old couch, a lamp, the toaster, the fact that light refracts off the toaster—all of it asks for an introduction to the baby, as you see it with her, and you think of what each of these phenomena are, or are for, and what they could possibly mean to a brand-spanking-new sensorium. The project is too great to hold in mind. Where to begin? How to offer what you know? An egg, a switch, a mirror and blue. What do these things do, and do to us? How does it all fit together?

We laid Tess in her bassinet. It had been Tracy's, an apple crate with cushions that Helen had sewn into the frame thirty-five years earlier. We had a drink, let our nerves sing for a bit, then everybody went to bed and imitated sleep. I listened like an animal to every snap and rustle, as if I was now prey to something large and dangerous. Tracy, too. She checked on Tess every few minutes, leaning over the edge of our bed to get a reassuring glimpse of the baby's breathing body, or to rebundle her wad of blankets. At three o'clock in the morning, every morning, we shared the same relief.

Phew. Downhill from here. Made it through another night. How three o'clock became the morning, I don't know.

Within a day or two everybody descended upon our house to view and coddle and talk about Tess. Everybody. For all I know, you were there, too. My parents, my siblings, Tracy's parents, her sister and family. My house felt like Woodstock. Our exhaustion doubled for it. So many voices in the kitchen, others in the living room. Nephews crashed toy cars under foot. Laughter upstairs and a phone ringing somewhere in the distance. Food, food, food. Where the hell was my kid in all this? I shoved a few plates out of the way and passed out face down on the kitchen table. A conversation between my mother and Tracy's continued over my head.

When our house emptied and settled, a new soundscape emerged. Daytime was like foreign travel. None of Tess's noises were native to our home. The glossary for her little cries, or snuffles, or peeps had yet to be translated. Her noises were generic, but all the more urgent for it, for their lack of meaning. Or, put it this way, she sounded like a baby, which was both adorable and inadequate. What did she want? We had yet to parse her cry into different cries, each directing us to something fundamental: clean me, put me to sleep, buzz off, feed me, touch me, stop this thing you call pain. Given the way her cries lit up the pain centres in our brains, we had to learn her vocabulary fast.

So we set about getting to know her. We hung out. I tried to pick up the dialect. But over the next few days something odd happened to me. Something, as from all blind spots, unexpected appeared.

Rather than Tess coming into focus, and that generic babyness dissipating as she grew familiar, rather than that, it actually persisted. It deepened. I couldn't find her for the babyness. I couldn't connect with her, though I tried and tried. I'd hold her, or rock with her, or bounce and walk about the house, and tickle her belly, all the things a papa does, but always crowding me was a sense of intervening fog. While I had a baby girl, and I loved her without limit, I had yet to feel she was my baby girl. I had yet to recognize Tess, whatever Tess meant.

What also persisted was a fear. The fear had been small and nagging at first, like a headache that needed a glass of water, or lunch. Just an ember in the skull. But whenever Tracy handed Tess to me, or Tess cried in her bassinet, or was inconsolable, or even when Tess slept peacefully on my chest during the small morning hours, which is among the greatest pleasures I've known, still something fanned that ember in my skull. The fear grew sharp and bright. Of what, I couldn't tell. It wasn't a fear of Tess, not exactly. I knew that much. But there it was, when we were apart, or when we touched. I couldn't name it, though I needed to.

My disconnection worried Tracy. She bathed Tess, sometimes in the sink, sometimes in the small plastic tub she'd set up at the kitchen table, but I just stood back and listened. Animals, they say, don't like to enter clearings, preferring to skirt the edges where thickets and trees provide cover, or quick escape. Nothing, I suppose, is quite as open and naked as a baby in the tub. The clearing in our home. I couldn't hug the walls close enough.

My remove became the norm. Tracy would have to ask if I wanted to hold Tess, which I would do gladly, but I rarely picked up Tess on my own. If I did, I asked Tracy's permission first, even before taking a turn at something as benign as time in the rocking chair. I behaved like a visitor, a friendly stranger, more than Tess's father. Why, I couldn't say.

It was two o'clock in the morning and Tess had been giving us the gears all night. Or maybe it was closer to five in the morning. Doesn't matter. Might as well have been noon. After a week in the fray, sleep deprivation teaches that a clock—even the cheap travel alarm on my night table—is actually a luxury item, and soon to be a souvenir of some bygone, childless era. Night and day are academic distinctions. Awake was awake, and that's all we knew.

Tracy rocked with Tess on the exercise ball at the foot of our bed, trying to soothe whatever enigma compelled her to cry, then cry a lot more, and quite regularly. I should pause to say—and this is my only advice to new parents—the exercise ball is your best friend. Got a Super Nanny? Good for you. She can play Mary Poppins to a tree stump for all I care. Just give me an exercise ball and your fussy baby. That nimbleness, and the menu of designer motions you can make with one, is really something to marvel. Up, down, side to side, rock, bounce, or sway, you name it. Bring it in the car, roll it from room to room and change vistas. It might be a rubber ball, but it is also the Cadillac of rocking chairs. What's more, you at least stay physically fit while your newborn pulverizes your psyche. Invest in one. Covet it. Hug it at night and tell it how you feel.

But the ball wasn't doing its trick this time.

"Here, let me take her," I said to Tracy, and got out of bed.

I tried to sound confident, even nonchalant, but my voice wouldn't go there. I'd have been about as calm if I'd asked Tracy to drop a live extension cord into my bath.

My arms snapped into cradle position, ready to take the baby, although "take" isn't quite the verb. I could safely "receive" but I couldn't actively reach for her. Nobody wants a blind guy actively reaching for them. Not unless they want to be blinded, too.

Tracy was determined to settle Tess, so she switched tactics, and began to pace around the bed and chant soothing phrases. I sat back and pretended that the phrases were meant for me.

Shelter from the crying was remote, even when Tess wasn't offering her many, although uniformly contrary, opinions. Her little wail had actually stained our eardrums. The effect was creepy. When she wasn't asleep, I could still hear phantom moans in the whir of our bedroom fan, or cries in the hum of the fridge. It was a similar phenomenon to the bad trips my friends and I had endured when we'd sampled the LSD on tap at our high school. I remember how we'd talked to the campfire, and how I'd heard advice coming from the menu at our favourite Denny's. Now I always heard Tess in the wind and the walls.

Tracy bounced harder and faster as she walked. I let my mind wander. That's the last self-defence strategy available to new parents, albeit a low-fi technique. Duck and cover under my school desk was about as effective against nuclear annihilation.

I wondered about some of the other parents I'd met. Specifically, I wanted to know the origin of the alien species that walks among us, and who or what are those mommies and daddies who always know their child's exact age, like Rainman to a pile of toothpicks.

"Oh, I dunno," they say all casual-like, "I'd have to guess that little Chewbacca here is, um, about forty-three days old. And eleven hours."

Whatever their colonial plans for our planet, screw them and their superior alien math skills. If they've got enough clarity of mind to bean-count the baby's age, I decided, they've got a nanny in the attic, and a pediatrician in the basement. And an extra brain hemisphere.

The situation in our bedroom escalated. Tracy outright pleaded with Tess for mercy. In answer, Tess explored the effects of friction on the human larynx. She'd finished nursing more than an hour earlier, too, so we were officially drifters in that darkest of territories, the rough and lawless seas between feedings.

"Seriously, let me try," I said. "I'll take her downstairs. Just see if you can get a bit of sleep."

"She can't be hungry," Tracy said. "She just ate, like, ten minutes ago."

"Minutes ago?"

Tracy unswaddled the baby and handed her over.

"Maybe she's too hot," she said.

"Could be. Could she be teething?"

"I dunno," Tracy mumbled. "I doubt it. Growth spurt maybe?"

We were whispering, as if we might wake Tess from her hysterical fit.

"Or maybe she's a bit gassy," I said.

Gas is the preferred explanation of the defeated. I might as well have suggested that Tess was possessed by the gods, or an ill-tempered howler monkey. When in doubt, all things puzzling can be blamed on gas. It's the ultimate ghost in the machine, and at the very most it offers a little reprieve from all the hopeless speculation.

Not that I was really a parent yet. For my money, parenting

is a title that's earned by the confident dispensation of phrases such as, "Don't put your finger in there," or, "Would you please, for the last time, take your finger out of there." By day five—or was it night eleven?—I was more like a novice auto mechanic at the corner gas station than a dad. When Tess was splayed on her change table, I'd stand over her, scratch my chin, and volley theories about what was really going on.

"Could be the socks. Maybe she doesn't like the socks."

"She's never liked swaddling, either," Tracy would remind me.

"True."

Scratch, scratch. I'd want to wipe my brow with the skull cap I didn't own.

"I still say it could be gas."

Tracy would agree. How could she not? "Goes without saying. Always could be the gas."

"Well," I would say finally, rolling up my sleeves. "Let's turn her over and see what she does."

The situation in our bedroom wasn't as accommodating. Finally Tracy conceded her need for sleep and handed the baby over. Tess's weight landed in my arms. Soon I heard a lamp click off and my weary gal crawl back into bed. The shape of my daughter wriggled with more determination, and a fresh surge of disgust.

A tiny bundle of pressure in my arms was almost the entire portrait I had of my daughter. She was mostly a combination of weight and movement that I cradled. The sliver of sight I had left in my right eye wasn't enough to let me glimpse her face. Maybe I'd catch a tiny patch of skin, or, if the lighting was good, I might squeeze the corner of an eye or a wisp of hair into my tunnel vision, but that was it. I couldn't see my face or her mother's blended there, in front of me, in a genetic equation of line and shadow that would have added up to somebody called Tess. The fact she was my daughter remained a story I told myself. An unnatural persuasion. Consequently, something else was lost, too, something in me. Her missing face felt like an obstruction to our bond, as if we were both reluctant to reveal ourselves. I'm not saying that blindness was an obstacle to love, but my body withheld from me something I imagined would feel more like fatherhood.

For that reason Tracy's pleasure and fascination stung. She could sit for hours—the calm ones—with her eyes pinned to Tess's face.

"It is the strangest thing," Tracy had said, "to see the two of us in a baby. Our baby's face."

Tracy always did her best to let me in on the secret, to let me experience what it's like to discover the two of us bound in another flesh. But the words didn't work. They don't. No magic conjured that deep identification. For now—and perhaps always, I feared—my first portrait of Tess would be a pressure in my arms, the smell of hair, and some sound. Babyness, not Tess. Nothing soothed me.

Nothing appeared to soothe Tess, either.

Back in the bedroom her fury grew. Her voice snatched and tore at her throat, so we darted down the stairs, slowing as we neared the halfway point. Like all babies, Tess had her pacifying quirks that could only be discovered by accident. Sometimes the enclosure of the stairwell relaxed her. Perhaps it was the echo, perhaps the simple jog of the stairs themselves. Whatever the reason, this spot in the house often distracted her long enough to catch her breath, which was long enough to remind her body that it could be a calmer one. We gave it a go.

No change in volume. Maybe we needed to hang there a bit, or jog up and down a few times. We gave that a try.

My stairwell tactic is predicated on the idea that a newborn is more than a baby. She is also an accomplished inventor. She transforms the most common household items into mesmerizing gizmos worthy of new patents. You thought you had stairs, but they aren't stairs anymore, they're fun. A vacuum, Band-Aids, the blow dryer, spoons, your housecoat and that bag of frozen peas, nothing is what it used to be. Any object—the incidental sound it makes and movement it encourages—has morphed into a potential tool for placating the baby. We'd even perfected a new application for Venetian blinds.

The stairwell wasn't doing the trick so we raced to the next stop on the circuit of comforts: Graceland. Yes, Graceland. I could speculate, but who's to say how these things come about? Tracy had tried the old record player a few nights prior. She wanted to see if some music could help soothe Tess's demons, or indigestion, or malaise or whatever. We didn't want to use the word colic yet, but it was on the tip of our tongues. The fear is if you say it, you might make it real, and real colic is a real shit-kicking for a really long time. Consider this: if you don't sleep at all, your day is in fact twice as long. That's just for starters. When parents say their child cried for an hour, it really means five minutes. That raises another blind spot. Babies, especially the crying ones, bend time. Thing is, they elongate it, particularly when you want less of it, not more.

Though we were into February, it just so happened that the last time we'd turned on the record player was back in

December. When Tracy first put the needle down, on came our Elvis Presley holiday collection. Immediately Tess clammed up. I'm told she even smiled. Could have been the gas, of course. Could always be the gas.

I didn't bother to flick on the light in the living room, which was typical, but also useful when trying to put Tess to sleep. Blind parents have at least that advantage. I groped for the stereo, and waited for the King to awaken from his vinyl slumber.

Tess paused. She listened. The quiet and the opening bars of "Blue Christmas" were so sweet. Music cleansed the air, while Elvis's voice carved order through chaos. Tracy will love me forever, I thought, as I pictured the smile on my baby's unknown face.

Then Tess erupted with extra vinegar, as if doubly pissed off at my cheap attempt to distract her. You know, as if to say, "What? You think all I need in this life is this one stupid record?"

I still had the rest of my arsenal, so we went back to work. We paced the hallway, then I sat her in her little chair and rattled some rattles, and squeaked some squeaky things. We attempted a round of swooping up and down, then astronaut steps complete with sound effects, but none of that worked, either. You can console yourself later that one day you'll introduce your child to selections of great literature, or expose them to cuisines that are thousands of years old. For now you have to pretend you're a monkey if that's what it takes.

My monkey impression scared the crap out of her.

Finally I planted us in the leather rocker, which I'd come to call "The Big Song Chair."

Tracy may have stumbled upon Elvis, but I had discovered another trick, and I'd kept it as my last resort, for just such a situation. Tess, I'd learned, would mellow if I sang any hurtin' blues song. The more hurtin', the better. Murder ballads were best. Anything about folks fixin' to die, really, or burying loved ones for misdeeds, then attending their own hanging, was welcome. Who was I to deny her brooding complexity? Her tastes were sort of worrisome, but it wasn't our doing. It's not like we'd blasted this stuff at Tracy's pregnant belly, the way some parents assault their unborns with Mozart. Baby Einstein has everybody's stereo doing psy-ops on the womb, treating it like Noriega's compound. No wonder ours is a generation surgically attached to its iPods.

Tracy tossed and turned upstairs. Immediately I busted out a tested ditty. Tess had, on several occasions, let me sing John Prine's "Sam Stone" to her for an hour. Something about the Vietnam vet experience tugged at her imagination. Or maybe she just admired that riff, "There's a hole in Daddy's arm, where all the money goes . . ." I began to sing in a low, calm voice, and even drew out the words "shrapnel" and "morphine" for her pleasure.

My monkey impression got a better response.

As I sang, Tess approached a new octave and intensity of shrieking. She doubled over with effort, and her ragged voice disappeared into a hoarse death rattle. Pockets of breath erupted without sound. The air caught in her throat like sandpaper on rough wood. She was sweating. I imagined red, a red face, if I could see the colour she was in.

The last thing I had to offer was a soother, if I could find one. For extra kick, we usually dipped it in gripe water, but I didn't know where the bottle was, nor did I know the bottle well enough to recognize its shape by hand. I didn't want to ask Tracy to fetch it, either. I wanted to do this on my own. I needed to. Fathers put soothers in babies' mouths all the time. Blind fathers should, too.

I pawed the dresser in Tess's room until my hand landed on a soft rubber nipple. As we were about to bolt through the doorway and back into the living room, my sense of space corrupted. Perhaps I turned too quickly, or too many times in my search, but I lost my positioning relative to the doorway, and with that I fell out of my map.

Blindness has taught me to move through space exclusively by memory, even in my own home. Rats navigate this way, too. Their movements are patterned, and the patterns are remembered by their muscles, not their minds. If a rat runs along the edge of a particular wall on a feeding route, and that wall is removed, the rat will continue to run along the phantom edge. Rats map the ghosts of bygone buildings. I move likewise through my home, habituated to its different turns and timing. That's why, if I move too fast, or lose track of my angle, I can actually become disoriented in my own home. I live in a habit, not a space.

This is why, as I bolted through the doorway carrying Tess and her soother, I clipped the threshold with my arm. And with Tess's little head. The sound was like the strike of a hammer on wood.

At that moment I was introduced to her pain cry, which I thought I knew, but had actually never heard before. It may have been her first pain from without. She was inconsolable. Me, too.

The ember in my skull felt at its brightest, and most searing, and suddenly I saw the fear for what it was. Tess, whom

I couldn't soothe, represented the greatest pain I would ever know, should anything happen to her, and worse, should I be to blame. Parents endure a constant, low-grade anxiety, it's true, but the love that fills us is made of equal parts terror. I wasn't afraid of Tess, but afraid of my love for her. It could, and will, hurt me one day, and so I'd stood back from it, so wary, so taken by self-preservation. I was in awe of this love. I was also ashamed of how I'd received it.

"I'm so sorry, Papa's so sorry," I pleaded as we sat on the couch.

Of course Tess couldn't tell me she was okay, nor could she forgive me. My own pain cycled through my body, as did hers, unable to find an exit. A sadness clung. I couldn't shake the thought that I'd hurt her. Didn't matter that it was an accident—I was the cause. My blindness had shown the smallest example of what it could do to her, and to me as a father.

I could hear Tracy getting out of bed, ready to intervene.

"We're fine, Trace," I called. "Go back to bed."

I laid Tess across my knees and tried to restrict her writhing. I couldn't see her mouth to put the soother in, so, gingerly, my fingertips lighted upon her face, and searched for her lips. Itsy, bitsy spiders.

"Shh, where's your mouth, punkin? Hold still, Papa needs you to hold still a sec."

But she wouldn't, and I was too afraid of hurting her to press the soother to her face.

"Please, punkin," I pleaded. "Please help Papa."

Again my fingertips swept for a picture of her mouth. She thrashed her head about until my pinky caught something damp. I recoiled, certain I poked her in the eye. She shook back and forth, and hollered until I was brave enough to touch her again.

Everything felt the same after that. Hers was a face without features. It wiped itself across my hand, and screamed. Then, in a flash of texture, I recognized the tip of her chin. It rose slightly from the roll of her neck. With my thumb and index finger I gently squeezed her mouth and tried to hold it still. Then with a quick jab, I tried to slip the soother inside. Tracy called from upstairs. Time was short, and the need to prove myself was greater than it should have been.

Just as I moved, Tess jerked away, and I stabbed the pacifier's tip into her cheek. Or maybe her temple, or worse. Tess was hysterical with pain. I pushed the rubber nipple into her face, and again it fell to the floor. Each time she grew angrier. Each time hurt us both a little more.

Tracy's feet thumped down the stairs. I could hear her heavy sigh approaching. Finally I picked the soother up and held it over Tess's face. One last try. A soother to a baby, a baby to a man. How can things so soft and small be so threatening? I cradled Tess. With my free hand I raised the soother, fingered the tip of all my love and frustration, pretended to aim, and plunged it into her. That hole in Daddy's arm.

I did it. Bull's-eye.

She spat it out.

"Damn."

Tracy arrived and took Tess from me.

"Did you try giving her the soother?" she said.

"I don't think she wants it. We, uh, banged into the door. Then I couldn't find her mouth to put the soother and . . ."

Tracy reassured me that Tess looked fine. She could see that I felt both incapable and dangerous. It must have been hard.

Tracy seemed so freighted, so tired, so on the front lines with Tess all the time. Occasionally she must have felt that I was somewhat incapable and dangerous, too. But here, in the small hours, at the limits of what I could offer, she reassured me that I would figure out how to do things, and that easier days would come. Within minutes Tess fell asleep in Tracy's arms.

Over the next few weeks I struggled to discover and to fix whatever was missing from my connection. But it was a puzzle. Maybe I felt all I was supposed to feel. That was a possibility, but an unsatisfying one. Where was the stupefying joy? Maybe the struggles of the first weeks, and all that worry, are the actual measure of the bond. Evolution might prefer it that way. Better to be cautious than to parade around drunk on joy while a puma gobbles up your baby. Persisting in me was a sense that I was an actor, an approximation, and one who wasn't entirely convinced he'd been properly cast as a father. Then I wondered if perhaps this was less an issue of identifying with Tess, and more about my inability to identify with myself as a parent. Around and around went the psychological Rubik's cube. Or maybe the answer was more obvious than I wanted to admit. Maybe I was just an asshole. Mystery solved.

One day I walked into the living room to find Tracy hovering over Tess. She snapped pictures with our digital camera. Tess relaxed on a white blanket on the couch, cheerful on a cushion. I can't recall if Tracy offered it to me, or if I asked to look at it, but I remember sitting down with the camera and straining to see Tess's face on the small display screen. No face. I just saw a field of white topped with some darkness, and a couple of lines like dead branches in the snow. One line suggested the divide of lips.

"Nope, I can't see her," I grumbled, and handed the camera back to Tracy.

She pressed some buttons to shrink the picture. Her hand placed my fingertip below the pixels that represented something Tess-like.

"See that?" she said. "That's her mouth there, and here," she moved my finger, "is her left eye. Can you see that?"

I found my fingertip, looked just above it and followed the path back and forth between the spots she'd identified. My brain began to infer what was missing in the spaces between, and that in turn made visual meaning of some of the other lines and shadows that orbited what I could now see as a little mouth. An eye. I saw a chin. I saw the chin and mouth at once, and then the eye.

"It's still a bit big for me."

Tunnel-vision asks that the world shrink enough to fit inside. No magnification, please. Tracy took another picture of Tess, this time from further away, then again from even further back. Again she mapped the face on the display for me, and again my brain pieced together the confetti until I could hold more and more of an image in mind. But I still needed it just that much smaller. If Tracy took a picture from any further back, the focus would be lost, and Tess's likeness would disappear altogether into a handful of pixels

Only one strategy remained to catch her. I pushed her away.

I held our camera's display at arm's length and stared at the tiniest speck of a face. She was no bigger than a dime. I could squeeze half of her face into my sight. And so I saw. Almost two months after she'd been born, I saw my daughter's face for the first time.

She looked like Tracy, and a face of my own I could barely recall. Something else, too. She also looked like—how do I put it?—Tess.

The fog lifted. Electricity surged through me. Every molecule in my body lit up and realigned itself. I felt more solid. Everything in me was held together by a bond I hadn't known before. Suddenly the ember in my skull, its fear, felt easier to contain and carry. I had a daughter, not a baby, not an abstraction or a blank in my mind's eye. Maybe because I wasn't born blind, I still had that old, sighted person's cognitive architecture, and its needs. I needed to see her, at least once. I needed to carry an image of her. Of us.

It had been just another one of those blind spots, I guess.

Attica, and Others

• • •

When I was twelve and my siblings each had fewer years than fingers, my parents bought a silver Chevy van. Ours was the deluxe comfort model with pleather and velour captain's chairs, tinted windows, wall-to-wall carpeting, and a fold-down bed in the back. The purchase wasn't anything kinky, just some solid parenting infrastructure. My parents, you see, needed a rumpus room with wheels, not a car. They had four kids. Four. Most people can't handle that many beers.

Seated behind my father, I would sometimes pretend to steer while fantasizing that one day I'd inherit the family van. Then I could jack it up and airbrush a battle scene from Conan the Barbarian on the side. Or a naked woman. Or Conan with a naked woman, together, in the back of our family van. But that fantasy went the way of my sight and my driver's licence.

Most of the time my siblings and I piled in with war-torn fury, fighting for dibs on the two captain's chairs. We'd squabble and torment one another until my father snapped. You knew you were done for when he bellowed his preferred phrasing: "Would you please—all of you—cut it the goddamned hell out!" Sometimes "Jesus friggin" made its way into his syntax, but I can't recall where.

That was our ritual on the road, except for the evening return trip, which was something else. Dad would bust out the John Denver, or maybe pop Jethro Tull's *Aqualung* into the tape deck. We'd drop one at a time, four fallen soldiers to the floor, passed out in a heap on the carpeting. What's a seat belt? One of the most delicious feelings my body has known is the drift to sleep while my parents steered us through the night. As I say, the van was smart parenting.

With such nostalgia in mind, Tracy and I decided to take a five-week-old Tess on her first road trip to Vancouver Island, where I had to give a talk. Maybe the distance was a bit of a hoof for a relatively fresh baby, but Victoria is only four hours away from East Vancouver, which is, in baby terms, two naps plus one stretch of wakefulness. A manageable equation.

When I became a writer, I began to measure time in word counts. When I was a smoker, I measured time in cigarettes. This would have been a half-a-pack trip, or fifteen hundred words of rough prose. Now, as a father, I measured the day as a series of scheduled show times and curtain calls for the baby. My mathematical units may change, but the math never lies. Our trip had good numbers, and all indications pointed to a smooth, reasonable journey.

Yes, well.

When Tracy buckled the car seat, Tess cried. No worries, I thought. Nobody wants to be buckled into this world. According to Tracy, Tess dug her little hands behind the straps and shook them like somebody behind prison bars. By the time we pulled away from the curb, Tess was in full voice, protesting her wrongful conviction. Or something.

All in all, a pretty normal takeoff. We'd only bothered with short car trips before, and Tess didn't seem to enjoy them much. A bit of guff at the beginning was to be expected. But we also assumed that Tess would acclimatize. She'd tune into the hum of the engine, and then the ride would ignite in her that deep and ancient nap that only children in cars know. What else could happen?

City gridlock happened. A lot of it.

Tracy grew up in the prairies, a buffet of long, open roads. I grew up in the suburbs. From the end of my cul-de-sac you could shoot a pellet gun down the street and not even graze a windshield. Or, well, so I thought. But here, now, by the third red light, it became clear that any belief Tracy and I had that cars help make kids sleepy was the product of our childhood landscapes, nothing more. A misleading rumour at best.

"This doesn't feel like normal traffic," I said. "Have we hit every red light or something?"

I was barely audible over Tess's screeching. The need to calm her with a good stretch of uninterrupted driving made city traffic a pernicious, alien phenomenon. I screwed up my face, a stranger in a strange land. We sped up, then we didn't any more.

"What are we stopping for?" I asked. I was in disbelief. "I don't remember there being a light here, or are we—where the hell are we?"

Tracy was busy singing to Tess, trying to calm things down. She didn't offer our coordinates between verses of "Itsy Bitsy Spider."

"This isn't Vancouver," I speculated. "This is Hell."

"I don't understand. It's a Tuesday," Tracy said.

"Hell only has Tuesdays, then. Tuesdays and red lights."

We sped up for a few seconds and stopped again. Tess continued to wail, so Tracy abandoned her and gave full attention to manipulating our way through the jam. Whether we sped or crawled, strategized, choreographed passes or pleaded with God or neighbouring cars, nothing made a lick of difference. We weren't getting anywhere, and Tess knew it. She was hoarse already. Finally I felt the car pick up speed. Hope swelled.

"Funny how Tess can make the red lights seem longer," Tracy said.

"No, it isn't."

She pumped the brakes a bit, trying to rock the baby to sleep, until, finally, we halted again.

"No, no stopping," I protested. "There wasn't a light here last week. I swear this isn't Vancouver."

The pain centres in my brain engorged. We were torturing our daughter, not bringing her along for a bucolic ride. I also worried Tess could deafen me at any moment. Tracy has always warned me that I've used up my disability quota in our marriage. If I lose so much as a fingertip, she's promised a quick divorce. Even if she has to leave in first gear on a Tuesday.

"My God," Tracy said as we stopped again. "This is useless."

"Maybe in the end I'll write something about our first road trip," I said, feigning optimism.

"Like what?"

I imagined a chapter with only the verbs "crying" and "undriving." It was very short. I dodged Tracy's question and just fidgeted with my air vent.

Tracy had one hand on the wheel, and had spent the past ten blocks in a contorted half-turn, her other hand fussing with Tess in the back seat, reinserting soothers, and spraying gripe water from a syringe. The smell indicated as many misses as hits. Tess sounded beyond retrieval from the dark side.

"Maybe we should just go home," I suggested. "Maybe this wasn't a good idea."

Tracy didn't answer. Her silence was hard to interpret, so I fished for something more.

"I mean, I know she'll stop crying," I said. "I just don't want you to feel you've got to go, you know, if you don't want to."

We had more than three hours to go. I tried to distort the fear my face was broadcasting, though Tracy was too busy to care how I looked, or what I thought.

I considered a quick cancellation call. I'd say the baby's sick or something. Nobody could grouse about that. To give up our road trip suited me in other ways, too. I'm afraid of riding in cars on a good day. Long ago blindness snatched any love I'd had for being matter in motion. You can imagine for a guy who hasn't run, skipped or even hurried in ten years how uncomfortable it is to hurtle forward trapped in a seat, my mortality in the hands of somebody else, those hands holding a little wheel, and the safe intention of that little wheel threatened at every moment by the unseen stream of hurtling others, and all of us kept apart only by some flimsy conformity—"Hey, let's agree that this here yellow line means something." Forget it. I'd rather go home. Or cry as you buckle me in.

Another minor trauma is the surprise of stops and turns. I'm talking about the most routine things. When you're blind, there's little indication of what is ahead. The world is unpredictable and sudden, even when the stop is slow and you know what's coming. I'm never ready for it to begin. I'm never ready for things to happen, or to finish, even the usual things. The soundtrack in our car is the hiss of wind as I suck it through my teeth, or my hand slapping against the dashboard as I brace myself for a collision with an imaginary beer truck, or the silent plunge from a cliff, or some quiet nothing, which is what usually happens. Like an infant, I'm in a place where the horizons have drawn themselves in. Neither Tess nor I can see what's coming, and neither of us can see what the distance intimates. It must have been painful and disorienting for her to first perceive time and space as we do. I know it's hard to let it go.

By the time we reached the freeway, I wanted to crawl into the back and soothe her, but Tracy and I both knew I couldn't measure out the gripe water. Other things were out of my repertoire. Helpful things. Even if I'd had a dose ready to go, I couldn't spray it in the right spot. Often I couldn't be within arm's reach without aggravating Tess further, anyway.

I don't mean to describe any of this to solicit anyone's pity, or worse, to express self-pity. My helplessness was just a fact. Lots of new dads report the same. Unfortunately, I also couldn't drive the car, pump the gas, or read a map. That left Tracy pretty much in charge of everything on our road trip except my air vent, which I continued to fidget with. Tess was already in a phase when only mommy would do, and who could blame her? Nobody likes a blind man banging them with a stuffed toy, or poking their person with a syringe and then asking, "That better?"

What remained in my power was good cheer, so I tried to find some. I patted Tracy's thigh. It was sticky with gripe water.

"She'll tire herself out," I promised. "Don't worry."

Tracy didn't seem to share my opinion. Neither did Tess.

Tess was only five weeks old, which also meant that I was only five weeks old as a father. The rudimentary knowledge I'd brought with me on this trip—along with the exercise ball for emergency rocking, two suitcases, a bassinet, a stroller and all the military cargo required for a single overnight trip with a baby—hadn't prepared me for the stamina of her protest. My little knowledge was too little for this.

I also didn't know that the word "infant" originates in the Latin phrase, "without voice." What I know now is that the person, or asshole, who came up with that definition didn't have an infant, or had never heard one in her car seat.

We eventually reached the ferry terminal, but waiting in line didn't help. Now we didn't have the engine's hum to muffle some of Tess's better surges. People in the cars around us experienced the full naked glory of Tess's tonsils, and rolled up their windows. Meanwhile, I felt like Marlow about to board his boat. Mr. Kurtz happened to be egging me on from the back seat.

And Tracy began to lose it.

"Fuck it, this is stupid," she snapped as she opened the door. "Maybe she's hungry."

"Could be. Do we have any Advil?"

"Or, I dunno, maybe it's gas."

Tracy said "gas" with its requisite hopelessness.

"Could always be the gas," I agreed. "Did we bring any Aspirin?"

"I just, I just don't know what to do for her."

Tracy climbed into the back seat, unbuckled Tess and began to breastfeed. It took a while, but a calm returned. That kind of nervous calm that vibrates, like a wet wineglass that rings when you rub it about the lip. The car also felt stuffy, the air stained with pungent dill from the gripe water. I opened my door to let a breeze through.

"What are you doing?" Tracy yelled. "Try closing that. I'm half-dressed back here."

Like her, I felt angry, and frustrated, and sorry. I heard looky-loos passing the car, making commentaries to one another, so I shot my best menacing face at them, as if to say, "Abandon hope, all ye who enter here."

Tracy and Tess were both quiet, so it felt like a good time to insert myself.

"Can I get you something?"

"Like what?" she snapped. "We're stuck in a car in a lineup for the ferry."

"Motrin?"

"We don't have any. Let it go!"

She'd been driving and caring for Tess, juggling nine things at once, all the way. Her every action illuminated our imbalance, and my reluctance to push myself. It was a stark contrast with her resolve and patience. She seemed very alone. I wanted to say it'll be okay, things will be fine. But I couldn't. I realized that I had no right. I hadn't any power to reassure her of anything because I was, so far, a bystander.

The silence between us, the sound we'd been trying to encourage, was unbearable.

"Do you ever feel like this was a mistake?" Tracy said quietly. "I'm not saying it is, but do you ever feel that way?"

She could have been referring to our trip, but I knew she wasn't. I pretended not to hear. Some things are better left unheard.

With the exception of those few minutes, Tess continued to wail until we reached the hotel several hours later. As we parked in the underground lot, her cry turned off with our headlights.

She smiled and bobbed her head for the clerk as we checked in, then convinced guests in the elevator that she felt pretty good about this world, not merely drunk on gripe water and exhaustion. We didn't even unpack the car. We headed straight for our room to try to put her down for a nap.

"See?" I chirped as Tracy unlocked our room. "I told you she'd tire herself out."

Like a seat belt, the door clicked shut behind us. A new cell. Take two. Tess gave the vocal stylings of Norwegian death metal a go. Those singers are not known for their naps.

We were going to remain busy, so I asked Tracy if she was hungry. We'd only forced down a few chicken fingers on the ferry, and that had been pretty much it for the day. I doubt that I need to combine any words other than "chicken" and "fingers" to explain how we felt.

"Hungry? I don't know," Tracy said, swaddling Tess.

"We could order room service or we could go out?"

"Where?" she said, but I knew she meant where would be appropriate with a nuclear baby.

"I dunno. Do you want me to phone down and ask?"

"Whatever."

"Do you want me to?"

Tracy didn't answer. She paced and bounced Tess. I knew she had a preference in there somewhere. Something would catch her fancy, and then I could get that thing she wanted. I phoned down and asked about nearby restaurants, places we could walk to, then recited the list and asked what she thought.

"I don't know," she said, a little dagger on the end of each word.

"You gotta help me out here, Trace. What would you like?"

Nothing.

She began to cry. "Why can't you just make a decision and stop asking me what I think? I'm tired, I'm hungry, I've been driving all day and feeding her, I'm covered in gripe water and puke, and all the stuff is still in the car. Just make a decision, that's what I want! Just do something!"

Tracy's fury inspired Tess to fan her own. This in turn made Tracy feel even worse and the two of them fed each other in a loop of sorrows.

The room shrank. We were locked in something smaller than my tunnel vision. I wanted to disappear. All perspective vanished. Every direction was a red light and Something needed to be done. Something unexpected, an act that would give Tracy both pause and reprieve because of its majesty and confidence and compassion. Standing in the doorway, fingering the "Maid Service" sign, I knew what I had to do.

I would unpack the car.

I snatched my cane off the scratchy bed cover.

"Where are you going?" Tracy said.

"Just give me your keys."

"What?"

Maybe she thought I planned to drive away, or grind along a wall in the parking lot.

"I'm going to unpack the car," I warned.

Down the hall I stormed, then pawed for the elevator call button. As I waited I mapped out where I was going in the hotel based on where I thought I had been. Not much came to mind. It was like trying to remember the face of somebody I'd never seen before. The most my synapses could serve up was an abstract chain of turns, an elevator and a couple of doors, most of which felt arbitrary, perhaps even borrowed from other memories of other hotels I'd walked through. I hadn't any idea where the car was, other than down.

In the elevator, my fingers traced two columns of flat, unmarked buttons. I pressed one at the bottom. An alarm went off. Manically my hands punched other buttons until the bell stopped ringing. Then I visited several floors above before the elevator finally took me down. Nobody seemed to notice the blind guy going for a ride.

To explore fresh territory, such as a laundromat, a broom closet, or a hotel lobby, a blind person must tap into the mind of a designer. As we walk we must intuit where doors might be, where walls likely belong, or where sitting areas might get in the way. Then there are the displays of Fabergé eggs—don't get me started on those—not to mention any number of banal surprises, such as potted ferns, windows, wet floors and decorative suits of armor that aim their lances at our nostrils.

Convenience would be most on the mind of an architect when designing an underground parking lot. People in hotels have bags and children, extramarital affairs and hangovers. They don't want to go very far. The exit should be dead ahead, and clear sailing.

I stepped off the elevator and into a wall. Two choices presented themselves: left and right. I chose left and walked into another wall. After backtracking five steps, I gave right a try. This architect clearly believed in equal rights, because that direction had its own wall, too.

Three walls, plus an elevator behind me, adds up to a small room, otherwise known as a box. Math doesn't lie. But the math didn't help me locate an exit. I slid my hands around at roughly handle height. No handles or knobs revealed themselves, nor any seams that would indicate a door. Nothing. I gave my exploration another go, methodical and slow. No exits, windows, pictures, fire extinguishers, riddling gatekeepers, dusty bones of previous captives, nothing appeared as I felt around and around my little Kafka obstacle course. I could take the elevator back, but what good would that do? Panic cinched itself around my nervous system.

Blindness has trapped me in very small spaces before. Its disorientation induces a funny logic. It can make you believe, truly, that doors have disappeared, or rooms have no exits, or even daffier things, such as, well, guess I'll just have to live here with the bank machines until they replace one of these windows with a door.

Now I was flat against a wall, my arms fanned, sweeping, trying to hug a two-dimensional plain, when a man opened a very flush door beside me. He paused, perhaps taken by my love for the wall.

"Are you looking for this?"

I didn't need to ask him what "this" referred to.

"Nope. I was just . . . looking."

I could tell, from the acoustics and damp concrete smell, that I'd finally stepped into the parking lot. One logistical problem solved. All I had to do now was find our car without setting off alarms or scratching up paint jobs with my cane. A far bigger and more complicated problem.

I took a step. I learned nothing. My feet took a few more steps. I learned nothing about our car's whereabouts.

"Fuck it," I mumbled, and pressed the panic button on Tracy's fob. The car alarm beckoned me to our suitcases.

It took about another twenty minutes to find my way back to the room, what with the elevator letting me off at different floors, and me slowly narrowing down which button belonged to the eleventh. As I wandered, pulling the first suitcase with one hand, caning with the other—a few more trips to go—a cruel memory bubbled to the surface. A guilt I've always felt but never understood.

Once, when I was seven years old, I woke up sick with a cold or flu. I remember a sore throat, and how I cried to my mother, not even heartened by the fact I'd get to stay home from school and watch deranged animation for preschoolers. What's not to admire about Barbapapa or Simon in the Land of Chalk Drawings? Even in high school I'd watch them. The mushrooms helped.

I doubt if I was crying because the pain was that unbearable, more that I was an unbearably wimpy child who was oversensitive to everything. I still don't know when it's appropriate to throw away birthday cards. Nevertheless, to soothe me, my mother offered a promise.

"Daddy's coming home from work," she said, "and he's got something for you!"

"What?" I said, imagining a dinosaur or a Superman cape. A functional one.

"You'll see."

I waited on the couch by the front door. My father worked graveyard shifts at a factory. Usually I got to see him at dinner, just before he went to work, or sometimes for a moment in the morning as he pulled in and we left for school. He was my hero, bordering on a mythical status, the way all things mysterious are heightened by their rarity.

When I heard his steel-toed boots clomp through the front door, I jumped from the couch, ready to receive my prize.

"What'd you get me! What'd you get!"

He palmed his pockets with exaggerated confusion. "What? I got you something?"

"You did! Mommy said you did!"

"Oh, right." He fished around in his jacket. "Put out your hand."

I did, and closed my eyes, savouring the last bit of surprise. He placed something in my open palm, something small and tidy, like a lighter. A hand-held flamethrower, perhaps.

"Have one now," he said, "and you can have another one later."

I opened my eyes to see a pack of cough drops.

I screwed up my face, the way I do when I'm pinched by disorientation, and said the phrase I've never let myself live down.

"That's it?"

My mother chewed me out, and sent me to my room. As was her custom she told me to think about what I'd just said, and to return when I could explain why it was wrong. I ran down the hall, sat in my room, and cried, not because of my initial disappointment, but because now I had a terrible picture in my mind. I nursed an image of my father working hard all night long, sweating in gloves and boots, just to earn the money to buy me some relief. In return, I threw it back and demanded something better. In my seven-year-old way, that's what I saw in my mind's eye. I'd dismissed what little he could do for me when it was the most that could be done. When it was plenty.

That feeling came home to roost as I fondled strange hotel doors, looking for the right number, listening for the inconsolable sound of my daughter. Again I'd been guilty of rejecting what little could be offered, only it was my little offerings that weren't good enough. To me, to be a father was always to be something large and heroic, just as my father had appeared. I'd sat in the passenger seat so far, letting most of my role pass me by.

But to unpack the car and to be able to tell Tracy that things will be fine—and to do these things for no other reason than they needed doing—could be heroic. I needed to ask that much of myself as a dad.

After I found our room and I'd made the three trips to bring everything up, Tess finally fell asleep in her bassinet. Tracy and I ordered up two Guinness and two chicken sandwiches. We lay in bed watching a TV show about little people. Apparently they're very happy and they overcome obstacles like nobody's business.

Tracy and I didn't have to say we were sorry. We just made fun of the show.

Our drive home the next day after my talk wasn't any different. Tess wailed the moment we buckled her into the car, and Tracy did what she could. At one point we pulled over to the side of the road, not even halfway to the ferry yet. She lifted the car seat out, opened up the handle, and swung the seat—baby and all—like a pendulum. Industrial scale rocking. She must have looked to passing traffic like a weary parent about to pitch her child into the woods. I sat in the passenger seat, as I do, only with a different sense of purpose and determination. I rolled down my window.

"Hang on there, babe," I said. "I'll catch."

Mr. Owb Goes to Town

• • •

Within the contract of marriage, a number of articles and appendixes are to be understood, though never spelled out in any detail, or said aloud. For instance, it's unspoken law in our house that I'm not to touch the tools. The prohibition extends its jurisdiction beyond our home. That's why my father gave Tracy—not me, his eldest son—a toolbox for Christmas. Inside were all the necessities of basic home repair: screwdrivers, vice grips, a level. Other stuff, I'm sure, but I've never been allowed to explore much.

The unique feature of Dad's gift was that he—what a guy—painted everything Barbie-pink. The drill, the hammer, the saw. Everything. Even the cool metal toolbox. He also tucked the pink spray paint can inside for touch-ups.

Some might have taken offence. Some might have interpreted the colour as a slight to Tracy, as if to say, "Behold the girly tools." But that wasn't the case at all. Of the few colours

I can still discern, pink remains the most vivid. What Dad's paint job really meant to do was brand everything "Tracy's tools" and, more important, broadcast the message, "Ryan, don't touch." Pink is my red light.

It was some sort of cosmic irony then, or perhaps it was simply an evolutionary defence mechanism, that Tess was, upon arrival in this world, pink.

Too bad I ignore pink. If Tess knew what happened to me the day I used the power drill, she'd have chosen another colour.

One afternoon I appeared in the TV room at the top of the stairs. I had a plan, and I was looking for my moment. Tracy was playing with Tess on the floor. There I could hear my daughter practising her only word. The one she'd invented.

"Ingy, Ingy!" Tess shouted, and a tower of blocks crashed.

Our theory was that Tess had conflated two common phrases into Tracy's name. Often we'd say to her, "It's Mommy!" and, soon after, "Are you hungry?" But Tess's ears seemed to have puréed our words into a more efficient caption: "It's Mommy" and "hungry" became "Ingy." It stuck as Tracy's new name.

I had yet to earn a name. For a while I thought I was "Aggie," then I thought I might be "Owb." But those disappeared. I was neither. I wasn't imprinted upon Tess deeply enough yet.

The problem, as I saw it, stemmed from a combination of interferences caused by blindness, by normal bonding circumstances, and by my own doing. We'd ratified a rash of new terms in our marriage, things I'm not to do, and with good cause. Feeding the baby was one of them. It's hard to earn a name without the ability to offer in return such a wondrous thing as breast milk. Despite the high levels of estrogen in our industrialized food supply, I remain far from developing functional breasts, and since we'd opted to breast-feed, Tracy kept that duty to herself. Not everybody would support our decision. Some New Age zealots advocate that new fathers should give their equipment a try. Seriously. If you let the kids go at it long enough, and hard enough, they say, eventually something good will come from the male breast, including more equality in the distribution of parenting duties. Could be. Enjoy. Other work was available, so I looked to it to help me earn a name.

Of all parental duties, changing the baby is the most equitable task, albeit a job with its own obstacles for a blind guy. I'm sure you think you can imagine, but you really can't. It's a more complicated and icky affair than just wayward fingers in the dip. You have only to behold the fucked-up origami that I pass off as gift-wrapping. Tracy's birthday present last year, the one prior to Tess's birth, gave her extra pause when she saw what I could do to a simple box. The trouble with wrapping starts when I give up on neatly folding edges. Instead I gather the festive paper into a sort of bag, twisting the top into a neck shape, then I tape the wad shut. I might as well have buried Tracy's new sweater inside a spitball. Say what you will, it hides the gift. Tracy graciously smiled as she dug her present out of its cocoon, but she also knew the baby could be next.

Tracy's boss was the first to note my unique challenges. A recent father himself, he mentioned on the phone one day that he'd tried changing his son in the dark just to see what my lot would be like. He gave up after he'd opened the diaper, which is to say he gave up before he began.

It's not impossible. I've changed Tess a few times, under supervision, but it was never easy, never totally successful, and never encouraging. The new diaper went on backwards, or sat too high, or sat too low, or was poorly hitched, or hung too loose, creating two diverting funnels, not a hermetically sealed catchment. Tess would writhe and cry, irritated by my slow, ham-fisted technique. My frustration matched hers. And these were only wet nappies. We weren't ready to test my skills with hazardous materials.

Part of the conundrum is that I use my fingers to "see" what I'm doing. Eyes let us know a lot at once, but hands don't. With my fingers I try to determine positioning, to orient my purpose, and to know what's going on in the meantime. To watch, in other words. But that doesn't leave any free fingers for the actual diaper change. Worse, I have to touch frequently, checking with obsessive-compulsive attentiveness to know if her legs have shifted, or if she's pitched herself at another angle while my hands were away trying to unfold a diaper, or to merely feel which way is front, back, inside and out. Sighted folks, of course, casually eyeball their babies and make faces or whatnot while their hands engage all the preparatory business. But as soon as I've taken my hands away, she's gone. I'm not watching any more. I have to put them back again to see her, and to see what I'm doing. Or not doing. It's a hell of a magic trick. I mean, just reread this paragraph and, hopefully, your brain will ache as mine does from such a small, unsophisticated series of actions. I'm here to say it's not a small action. It is a series of super-complex and frustrating movements better suited to Peking acrobats.

As I say, I've made it through a few, but the first time her diaper was full of poop was the last I saw of it. I held up a baby wipe, blankly stared at Tess's bottom, and said to Tracy, "Okay, where should I put this?" I never got to my next question: "And now, how should I move it?"

Tracy has never begrudged the fact that she has changed all but maybe three or four diapers. I doubt Tess has either. It was agreed, then, albeit unspoken, as so many of these things are, that I would make myself useful in other ways. What those would be was another matter. Certainly I could try to bathe her or dress her or a host of other daily necessities, but we also agreed that Tess shouldn't have to suffer dirt, rashes and fashion embarrassments just to prove my independence. Not with Tracy around and able to see.

What we noticed, with a degree of discomfort, was that our progressive household, and its gender equalities, was changing. Reverting, really. For years, say, I'd made it my pleasure to do a lot of the cooking. Sure, I was painfully slow at it, but smell should be the primary guide to a good taste. That seemed within my skill set. So, the olive oil flew, and the kitchen was mine while Tracy continued to add to her toolbox, or drove the car to buy paint and rollers when needed, or Drano to fix my handiwork at the kitchen sink. In other words, my blindness made the dismantling of domestic gender stereotypes easy. But when Tess came along, all that changed. Quickly we morphed into a 1950s model of parenting: Tracy did the mom stuff, the childcare and its hurricane of activities, while I wrote every morning in the basement to bring home a little more cash. Tracy cooked Tess's purées, and I let the kitchen go. Too much needed doing to accommodate my pace. Then there were the diapers and the threat of my need to assert any independence through them. I just focused on providing financial security. Ick.

Ironically, though, such a reversion of roles was our new form of a progressive family. While I was like an old-fashioned dad, I was also a blind dad, a gainfully employed blind man, which is rare enough, and that suited our dynamic and its limitations best. Family first. Still, the bulk of labour fell on Tracy's shoulders, and so in many ways Tracy's role doubled, while mine diminished. Then her responsibilities grew again when she went back to work the following year, and still retained all the mom stuff to do with what time remained. How do women do it? I can't even boil water while I'm peeling the potato.

How I could best help out, and be a father at this stage, wasn't my puzzle alone. Tracy's fears mattered, too. It's one thing to become a mother, to be a new mom, and to have the uncertainties and doubts that go with so much of that overwhelming responsibility. It's another thing, then, on top of it all, to hand your defenceless baby over to a blind man. Who'd let that guy try his luck at a few new tasks? What mom would do that, even if the blind man is her husband? It goes against many instincts. As Tracy wrestled risk and responsibility in her own mind, I grew frustrated, feeling I couldn't find anything even I was comfortable doing. Tess and I had yet to be left alone. I'd snuck more time with the pink power drill.

So I decided one day to start a quiet revolution. In the TV room, I waited at the top of the stairs and listened to Tracy and Tess play. Another tower of blocks crashed. Tess's favourite game. I could help her with the knocking down part, but sucked at finding the blocks afterwards. One round of destruction did not add up to much of a game.

"I think I'll take Tess for a walk," I announced, and held up the harness for the Baby Bjorn carrier.

Tracy paused. The silence throbbed with concern. "Oh," she said, "uh, okay."

"I've got the Bjorn here if you can put her sweater on or whatever."

"Uh, you sure?"

I was already busy putting the harness on inside out. "Yep. We'll be fine."

"I'll go with you, then," Tracy said. She sounded extra cheerful. Persuasive.

"Well, if you don't mind, I'd really like to take her myself. Maybe you could do something nice while we're gone."

"Like what? I like playing with Tess."

"I dunno. Yoga? Coffee? Or maybe, uh, yoga?"

I couldn't recall how we'd spent an hour of our old lives.

"Oh, oh," I brightened, "or what about Facebook! You could change your status and stuff. Whatever it is you guys do there. To each other, or whatever."

"Naw," Tracy insisted. "I'll just go for a walk with you two."

I couldn't angle a kind way to say, "But I don't want you to walk with us. I want to put our baby in danger all by myself." Best to deflect the issue, I decided.

"Look, all I'm saying is that you never get any time alone. I'd like you to have some. That's all."

Tracy didn't need reminding. In months she'd never been further than the shower without Tess either in her arms or in sight. Compound that with feeling the claustrophobia that comes with marriage to a blind guy. I'm always holding her elbow. Walking, for Tracy, had evolved into an imitation of an agile Christmas tree, baby, purse, diaper bag and husband dangling from her limbs like the jolly bobbles we are.

Tracy continued to stack the blocks for Tess's levelling hand. She massaged a few worries.

"Are you sure you can—"

"Yes, yes," I said.

"But, what if, what about . . ."

She couldn't bear to finish the thought. That or she couldn't pick one possible catastrophe from so many.

"Relax. We'll be fine." I could feel myself bristling at her anxiety. "It's just a little walk. We'll be fine. I know my way around the neighbourhood. You know that."

I struggled with the clasps on the carrier. Tracy's reaction had already infected my confidence. She stayed quiet for a moment, then gave herself over to my first walk. It had to happen eventually.

"You have that on upside down," she said, and got up to dress the baby, maybe for the last time.

A few minutes later I descended our front stoop with Tess. I have never been more petrified as a blind pedestrian. Tess was strapped to my belly. The weight of her there, that new presence against my chest and stomach, brought other sensations to the surface. I could feel memories of mushing my gut into any number of undetected obstacles. Into poles, into bicycles, into parking meters, into chain link fences, into parked cars, and into, God, you name it. I've even tested the conviction of street performers who pretend to be mute robots. You know, the ones who come to life when a coin drops into their hat. One guy saw me coming, but remained a human statue until it was too late.

Such mobility risks never bothered me much because the gamble of ramming my body about the world has always been my own. Now I had a small, human bumper, the kind that might not survive any errors.

I stepped cautiously, deliberately, as if carrying a sack of sweaty dynamite. I swept my cane with the care of a mine detector. Twenty minutes later we'd made it to the corner of our street. As you might expect, this was no fun. No walk in the park. The first person to pass us saw the situation in simpler terms.

"Jesus, that's gotta be tricky," she said as she passed.

Maybe she said it to me, or maybe to a person she was walking with. Or maybe to her pal Jesus, as her phrasing suggested. Already strangers were praying for our survival. Within the next block, and the next twenty minutes of slow-going, at least half a dozen others offered similar prayers, or insisted on guiding us, or asked to take us home, or asked if we'd lost mommy.

It's a small thing, but only then did it occur to me what we looked like. Because I don't see other people breezing by, scratching their crotches in public, or whatever it is sighted folks witness on a street, I forget that I have an image. Ours wasn't the one a new father hopes for. Despite Tess's devastating cuteness, despite her lime-coloured, rave-baby sunglasses and flower booties, despite her drooling open-mouthed grin and despite whatever that magical power is that babies possess to elicit coos and peculiar warbling noises from the most curmudgeonly of strangers, so far folks could only see her vulnerability with me. It saddened me. I suppose it's like trying to show off your infant daughter when folks can't see past the fact you've got no hands. There isn't a sailor costume cute enough to distract from that.

A small narrative took shape in my mind. A six-year-old Tess asks if her friend can sleep over. Unfortunately Tracy is out of town, so when her little friend's dad knocks on the front door, ready to drop off his child for the night, he is greeted by a blind man. My reluctance as a father would be the same, too.

Slowly we edged around the corner at Grant Street, and left the residential sidewalks. My daughter and I were about to try the crowded thoroughfare of Commercial Drive. More people meant more noise to govern by. A good thing. As well, the sound of traffic stretched into the distance, so at least I had something pointing me in the right direction. The help of crowds has a backhand, though. Busy people pay less attention to their surroundings. Folks regularly clip my shoulders, and sometimes I'm knocked down, caught off balance. Here, they might even bump us head on, or smush a slice of hot, cheap pizza into Tess. There would be dogs, too. Usually it's pit bulls around here. Often they're leashed to bike racks or snoozing in front of doorways, as you'd also find them in their native habitat, by the gates of Hades. Too often I've whacked my cane against a dog where no dog should be expected. Too many times large, toothy shadows have growled and snapped at my legs. Tess could become a chew toy.

I waved my free hand in front of us, braced my arm, and pushed ahead, the way running backs rush into a dog pile, but really, really slowly.

Within ten steps somebody clipped my shoulder. As I rebounded, it happened again, this time sending me off course, towards a garbage can. Tess's legs grazed along its concrete casing as I turned and reoriented myself. She began to fuss. Her fear was legitimate and showed foresight. The only defence I had left was my cane, so I tapped hard and loud, not because it worked better, but because I figured the noise would part the way, or at least wake up sleepy folks. It seemed to work okay, too. I made it one block without further incident. The only thing I missed—that I know of—is that Tess had tossed her baby sunglasses aside. A woman caught up with us. She'd retrieved them from the tomato bin outside Norm's Fruit and Salad.

"Here," she said, "you let the baby drop these."

"Thanks," I said, "but, really, I just didn't see."

"Sure, whatever. You should be careful."

"Right. Good point."

Maybe she worried that the thought hadn't crossed my mind. Either way, telling a blind person to be careful is like telling us to look out. We're mostly trying to figure out how to do it, not whether we should.

I thanked her again and tried to fit the glasses back onto Tess's face. Her mouth and hands felt damp. Viscous.

"That would be spit-up," the woman clarified.

My hands slid down the front of the carrier, and traced a lengthy slick. Tess gurgled and kicked. She'd found her own way to part the crowd.

I didn't have a cloth, so I decided to stop in at the café at the end of the block to get some napkins. Or steam-clean us with the wand on the espresso machine. As we approached, I recognized a voice from one of the sidewalk tables. It belonged to Milo, an older Italian man who continues to be, as best I can determine, shackled to the café.

"My God!" he said as we approached. "You got-ta little baby!"

I envied his voice. It piped through a megaphone, not a larynx. I heard his chair slide across the concrete as he stood. He was up and at us in seconds, and pinching Tess's chubby cheeks. This was a man who looked past my state and her vulnerability. He simply drank in the baby and her babyness, puke be damned. It was refreshing.

"Aw, so beautiful! Lina, come outside! Lina come and-ah see the baby!"

Lina, the café's owner, shouted back from inside. "What baby? Whose baby?"

"Who cares? It's a baby!" he shouted, and resumed work on Tess's cheeks.

Lina pounced, gushing, kissing Tess's feet and tugging for affection. I tried to steady my balance. My café friends were a gale-force wind.

"I'm telling you," Milo said, coming up for breath. "This, this is a helluva beautiful baby. Bella! Me and-ah you, we could have had a baby like this, Lina."

"Don't you think like that! I'm a married woman!"

Lina always spoke with exclamation marks.

"And even if we were married," Lina continued, "and even then if I let you have a baby with me—which I wouldn't—this would not be it! This, this baby could not come from you! Me, yes, you, no!"

"Ingy?"

"See? She says my name! She likes me," Milo said. He tickled the baby some more, presumably in the dry spots. "And, look, she got her little sunglasses on and—ah—"

His megaphone dropped. All the espresso-fuelled joy drained from his body.

"The glasses. My God, no," he said, his voice low and serious. "She don't see! My God. She don't see, like you!"

It took a few minutes to convince him that everything was fine. He couldn't believe that babies might wear sunglasses for comfort, not to terrify friends.

Lina wiped Tess down, and stuffed a brick of napkins in both my pockets before we left. I'd had enough, so I thought now was as good a time as any to head home. Why push our luck?

As we rounded the corner at Graveley Street, stepping past the pub and U-Brew, a mere thirty yards from home plate, the ridiculous girth of an SUV shot out from the building's underground parking lot. The weight of its super-sized engineering, and Freudian neurosis, blew across the sidewalk in front of me. And hit us.

The vehicle brushed close enough to bat the cane from my hand and into the street. Maybe I couldn't walk the baby. Maybe I couldn't walk.

My heart stopped. Tess lost all composure, and who knows what else. I didn't know if she'd been clipped. Everything happened so fast. She sucked wind, readying a hail of tears and a permanent distrust of her father's guidance. Nothing came, though, and still nothing came, so I knew she was shaping that worst, silent, open-mouthed cry—the deep cry, the one that can't find any voice in the beginning. I braced myself for the SUV about to roar from her mouth. Then it arrived.

She violently shook and kicked and squealed with laughter.

Out of her came a glee powerful enough to start my heart again. A laugh like I'd never heard before. Meanwhile, the driver had stopped. He fetched my cane. It was a little more bent than usual. Had I been one step closer to home, my cane would have resembled what would have remained of my spine.

"Sorry there," the driver said, and handed me my new boomerang. "Didn't see you coming."

Before I knew what to say, or remembered how to yell, he was back inside his tank, putting it in hyperdrive. I had to wonder why his vehicle wasn't pink, like everything else in the world that I'm not supposed to touch. Through his open window he shouted a parting message.

"Cute baby," he said, and sped away, taking several years of my life with him.

Tess continued to laugh, unaware anything mortal had happened. Either that or she already appreciated the irony of her invisible, blind father. After all my caution, turns out that my risks could be her joy. We'd forged a new bond. We were daredevils of a unique kind. We would go for many walks. Papa was super fun.

"C'mon, punkin," I said, and resumed our cautious pace. "Let's go see Ingy before somebody else doesn't see us."

"Owb," she said, and kicked a little.

I think she meant it, too.

The Sound Effects

• • •

What's that?" I said, and cocked my head into my alarmed position.

"I didn't hear anything," Tracy said.

I knew the subtext of her tone. She'd heard exactly what I'd heard, but was pretending she hadn't. An ineffective technique to make real-world phenomena go away. Some call it denial. Others call it hope.

Most evenings in our house looked the same. If you'd peeped through the kitchen window, you'd have caught Tracy sitting next to me, both of us in Guinness therapy, or folding a basket of laundry, but lending most of our concern to a plastic orb on the kitchen table. Like most orbs—especially the plastic ones—ours had futuristic pretensions. All baby monitors do. The designers want to reassure new parents that a future is out there, and that their babies will be part of it. In the meantime, our job was to receive the monitor's foreign language dispatches. Not only did most evenings in our house look the same, they sounded the same: indecipherable.

"You didn't hear that? It was some shifting," I said.

"That was me. That was my chair."

"No, it came from the monitor. That's why you shifted in your seat. You were leaning in to hear it."

"No, I wasn't," she said, and leaned back, away from the monitor.

"Damn. She's waking up."

I took a long pull on my beer and braced for trouble. If Tess was already surfacing, it wasn't clear if, or when, or how she'd go back down. Ever. Tracy's chair creaked a little.

"Did it sound like that?" she said.

"No. It was a quick and shifty sound. Like blankets moving."

"You probably heard yourself breathing through your nose. You do that when you study the baby monitor."

"What are you talking about?" I said. Or whined. Probably through my nose. "I'm not studying anything. I'm just listening."

"So hard that you're staring at the speaker."

Tracy was right about my fixation. A lot was at stake. For weeks, Tess had been in the habit of waking up every hour or two. We were desperate for her to experience just three unbroken hours of sleep, which happens to be the minimum ration necessary for an adult's survival. The goal was to keep the house as close to womb-like conditions as possible, but even quieter. A womb within a womb. If we weren't cowering in bed, we sat at the kitchen table, afraid of every noise we made, and those our daughter made. Or didn't. Who could tell?

After Tess refused to snooze longer than a sitcom, everything in our house seemed to amplify and to wake her. It wasn't the baby monitor's fault. Pick up a dish towel too abruptly and the ruffle could kaboom two floors up. I moved in slow motion, and with exaggerated precision. Mine were big, soft steps. Like a mime's, but even quieter. The stairs didn't creak any more, they popped like firecrackers. Light switches didn't click on, they exploded in my hand. At times I caught myself debating if I really needed to put my beer down at all. Quieter just to carry it around the house. I already did that with the dog, who might otherwise bark. The pug remained pinched in my armpit like a football.

For all our silence, we suffered some unfortunate side-effects. Our friends noticed that Tracy and I mumbled something awful. We hadn't used our voices properly for most of the summer. My diaphragm shrivelled, and to this day, as indicated by the frequency of my students' asking me to repeat myself, I still haven't recovered.

But I didn't just stare at the monitor. I didn't merely cling to a hope that Tess was asleep. I worked hard. I was convinced I'd figured out how to project my thoughts into the digital receiver, then use it as a platform to burrow commands into Tess's brain. Some people call this condition telepathy, and others call it sleep deprivation. I called it hope. I simply knew that if I didn't pour my will into the baby monitor, I couldn't enforce the family mantra, "Stay down, stay down." Mine was the only power keeping Tess asleep.

"You know what?" Tracy said. Her tone was sheepish. embarrassed. "Sometimes I catch myself trying to will her to stay asleep, and I'm convinced it works. Isn't that weird?"

"Totally. That's cracked."

Tracy mumbled something else, but her mind sounded far away, the messages delayed by distance travelled. I heard the laundry basket slide across the table and Tracy's head thunk down in its place.

" . . . and maybe going crazy. I need some sleep," she finished.

I fished for a response to her half-statement, something supportive.

"Don't worry, you're not telepathic, babe," I reassured her. "I am."

My beerless hand dialled up the volume on the monitor, but it proved to be fully cranked. That wouldn't do. Without any extra oompf, I couldn't detect further evidence that Tess had been stirring a moment ago, or was now waking up, or was in distress, or was in pain or, most likely of all, was struggling to roll over and free her airway of the soother that had broken in two and lodged itself sideways in her throat. That was the sound I'd heard. I'd never heard it before, but I knew it was that sound. Tomorrow we would pick up an equalizer and some decent speakers.

"Oh, you're right," Tracy said, and picked up the monitor, as if she could see what was happening. "I just heard it."

"Heard what?"

"You're right. I think she's waking up."

"I didn't hear anything."

We stared at the monitor for signs of life. I heard nothing this time.

"See?" Tracy said.

"Me? No."

"There it is again. I should go up."

"No, you'll wake her!"

"But I'm sure—"

"Don't go in there!!"

"I just heard—"

"No, you didn't. That was a car passing by the window. Trust me."

"I'm going up to check on her."

The only thing worse than Tess waking up was accidentally waking her up. I snatched the monitor and put it to my ear. If Tess was tapping code against the crib rails with her soother, dammit, I'd piece it together. I'm a blind guy. This was my turf. I listened carefully for a few seconds, then pronounced judgment.

"You're hearing the fan," I concluded. "It's got that uneven sound."

"Are you sure?"

I put the monitor down and relaxed my power.

"Babe," I said, "I know every sound in this house. That's the fan. She's not stirring."

Tracy made her scoffing noise, a sort of nasal bluster of disbelief. Usually it occurs seconds before she's right about something.

"Sorry, but you do not know every sound in this house."

"Do, too."

"Nuh uh."

"Oh, yeah? What about the time I got the neighbours out of bed? I woke up in the middle of the night because I heard their smoke detector. From next door."

I'm tuned to irregularities. Even distant ones that have nothing to do with me.

"You smelled burning plastic," Tracy said, "and that was because they lived below us. You didn't hear anything. You have terrible hearing, Mr. I Spent a Decade in Night Clubs in Front of the Speakers."

I pretended not to hear that.

"There it is again," Tracy said.

"You mean that swishy sound?"

"Yeah."

"That's the fan. I told you."

"Did you turn it on?

"No."

"Me, neither."

In my mind's eye, my agile body raced up the stairs to confront who, or what, had turned on the fan I'd so correctly identified. In reality I shuffled into Tess's room and snuck a closer listen. What I discovered was an airy, still nursery, which sounds an awful lot like a fan, or a stirring baby, when processed through a highly sensitive microphone. What Tess heard, and what made her cry, was her tone-deaf father trying to find the doorknob on his way out.

Some parents have a hard time adapting to the inevitable clutter that comes with a baby. Piles of towels and spit-up rags. Strange toys, designed by Dr. Who, light up, sing about farmers or the colour red, then shoot imaginary death rays at your face as you trip over their steering wheels. Infestations of soothers occur. Whenever I put my blind man's hand down—on my desk, to my plate, under my pillow—I palmed a rubber nipple. It's a peculiar surprise, to discover your home has been remodelled with teat-like surfaces. I can't imagine what our house looked like some days, but Tracy was fastidious and never let it get out of control. It's in her tidy nature, but she also kept things predictably placed for me because I needed the stable spatial layout in order to survive. Tess, too.

As I marched through the living room and carried the baby, Tracy ran ahead, clearing the way like a curler with a broom.

But in the same way that the visual quality of a newborn's house grows more crowded and complex, so does its soundscape. The baby monitor was just one of the many new phenomena that filled my ears and made little sense. That's not to say I couldn't appreciate the gizmo. I'm all for parenting innovations that lack visuals, and I'm all for technologies that augment the capabilities of the human ear. The problem was, of course, that just because the microphone allowed us to hear more—including the neighbour's flushing toilet, and Tess's spazzing eyelids during her occasional REM sleep—that didn't guarantee we could understand what the hell the monitor was picking up. Nevertheless, I enjoyed that Tracy's body and my own were on equal terms and had identical abilities between the hours of tubby time and first light. All parents are part-time blind folks. Every night, in fact.

The reason for the baby monitor's invention resonates in its design. Called the radio nurse, it was created in response to the kidnapping of the Lindbergh baby in the 1930s. Yes, I researched the origins of baby equipment. (Consider what *you'd* look up if your day were twenty-three hours long.) Anyway, the ability to quickly replace a lost soother or to calm every whimper and stir wasn't the intention of this radio nurse gizmo. Paranoia drove its engineering. Paranoia. That I understood. The backhand is, of course, that although the monitor was supposed to relieve worry, it powered a fresh range of parenting terrors. At night, Tracy and I scared ourselves stupid listening to the radio nurse the way families in the 1940s must have gathered around to appreciate real radio programs. No episode of *The Shadow* is more spooky or disturbing than the program I came to know as *The Quiet Baby.* A brilliant script. Nothing happened. Nothing but a prolonged silence. Every parent will tell you that silence is more sinister and loaded with calamity than a crying baby. At night, if Tess slept, we listened and debated about what was not going on, while a horrible tension built, one that intimated catastrophe any second. Fantastical scenarios revealed themselves. I prepared myself for an adult voice to suddenly cackle from the monitor while we were in the basement updating the family blog. Or, worse, the quiet might continue a little too long, a little too quietly. Jesus. Gives me the willies just thinking about it.

Before Tess could talk, many of my alarming experiences as a father were related to monitoring of one kind or another. Surveillance is typically eyeball duty, but my primary tool had to be my ears. Not everything smells like trouble, and you can't keep a hand on your kid at all times. Besides, Tess made hundreds of sounds. That's why my ears and nervous system went into overload, growing as hypersensitive as the baby monitor itself. My mind evaluated, reconsidered, then deconstructed every wavelength available. Listening in our house drew on all my postmodernist education.

I should clarify here that the rumours aren't true. Blind people don't hear more. We just hear differently, listening for different information than sighted folks. We pick up sounds that suggest visuals we'd expect to have seen, such as the smile that accompanies a tone of voice, or the mouthful of dead leaves a toddler has picked up at the playground and is speaking through in peculiar, muffled tones. The blind listen when others watch. Too bad the pictures aren't always clearly audible.

Case in point. Tess was new to her high chair, and equally new to food that didn't come from her mother. When she was about six months old, we started with simple purées, as we were instructed, and added a new fruit or vegetable every four days. Fine. By the time she got to bananas and tofu—a meal that makes more noise when it is slurped and gummed than any other—I finally learned that the *mmm* sounds she made didn't just mean "yum," but could also indicate "Hurry up with that spoon," and if her tone wavered, it could also mean "Go away and stop trying to jam that spoon into my forehead."

We'd also read that chewy things were good for teething. That cruelty had finally begun. A completely boneheaded evolutionary process, if you ask me. Intelligent design? The ninny who decided that babies should go through so much oral pain just to have the damned things fall out and grow again gets an F in my class. The ensuing drool turned Tess's face and chest and legs into a viscous slick. Her use of "mmm" also pushed the drool out of the way, so it had even greater functionality as a sound than just a stab at meaning.

Among those chewy things we'd read babies could gnaw for relief, the heel of a crusty baguette seemed the most appealing. After dinner one night, Tracy lopped off a decent chunk and gave it to Tess. Tracy asked me to watch the baby and the rock-like bread while she cleared away dishes. In our house, "Watch this, Ryan," means I'm supposed to listen, and, when in doubt, touch what I'm trying to listen to. I gave it my all. As you can imagine, listening to saliva dampen bread is about as revealing as listening to a sunset change colours.

Tess did her gumming, which didn't make much sound, and she dropped crumbs on her tray, which made even less sound. I watched, but what I didn't hear was Tess gathering everything into her maw, stuffing herself with all the orphaned debris she'd mashed and liberated. She packed her cheeks. Ten pounds of mud into a five-pound sack. All I heard was the gentle, benign glups of drool and the occasional "mmm." No need to touch for reassurance. When her mouth was full, she gave swallowing a try. Basically she forced a bakery truck down her esophagus. Next thing I heard was nothing at all. I heard contentment. Digestion. Perhaps I heard thoughtfulness. Maybe I heard a closed mouth, maybe a smile.

And those all sound the same as choking.

Tracy turned around and saw that Tess couldn't breathe. The next thing I heard was Tracy lunging across the room and whacking Tess on her back. Hard, but not hard enough. That whacking sound I recognized all too well, and suddenly I parsed the excruciating quiet coming from my daughter. I didn't know what to do. I knew what Tracy was doing, but it didn't sound hard enough to me. I could feel in my own body the contradictory impulses: Tess needed a solid thwack on the back to dislodge the bread, but how do you hit your baby?

"Hard!" I shouted. "Whack her! Harder!"

Tracy by this point had snatched Tess out of her chair and was dangling her upside down. I'd caught that much but not any or enough hitting going on.

"You gotta hit her!" I shouted, but heard nothing. Maybe, like me, Tracy was paralyzed by the idea. "Harder!" I reminded her.

The silent picture was actually quite busy. Tracy had wedged her finger in Tess's mouth and excavated a crusty heel the size of a golf ball. Don't worry, the books had said.

Your baby will chew with gusto. It's good for them. Perfectly safe. Of course, these books assumed somebody would be watching, too.

"You gotta tell me what's happening," I said. "What's going on?"

Tess began to cry, more startled than hurt, and I'd never been happier to hear her so upset.

At breakfast the next morning I had toast while Tess gummed a rice cracker. Things were quiet. Too quiet. I listened, but couldn't hear over all the crispy toastness going on in my mouth, like some demolition derby of the skull. For her safety I'd have to switch to gruel. Or eat her breakfast. Instead I chewed, then stopped and listened, then snuck a few quick chews, then stopped again for reconnaissance. This is not a healthy way to eat.

Tess's silence deepened. I panicked.

"Tracy! Tracy, she's—!"

I dropped my English muffin, leapt up and readied my hands to reach down my daughter's throat.

"No, she's not. Relax," Tracy said. "She's smiling at you."

Tracy spooned pear glup into Tess between surges of baby "mmm's." A bit went down the wrong pipe, I guess, and when her sputtering happened to coincide with her joyful kicks in the high chair, well, you can imagine the picture in my mind. I saw her face turning blue and her joyful kicks as spasms intended to loosen the death grip of murderous pear goop.

Again from my mouth shot my alarmed half-phrasing, "Tracy, Tracy, she's—?!"

"Jesus, she's fine," Tracy said. Her tone was exasperated. "She's just coughing. Relax. Babies cough."

I sat down, uncertain what to do with all the adrenaline I'd accumulated in the past five minutes. I thumbed the edge of the table, fidgety, and noticed that it felt unnecessarily sharp. The dangers of our house coalesced in my mind's eye. I'd never really seen them before. The corners of the table hovered at toddler-face level, crisp and defined, not unlike the corners of the chairs and sideboard and coffee table, as well. I conjured the layout of our house. The coffee table and its pointy bits happened to be at the foot of a few stairs descending from our kitchen. All the pointy bits were ready to pierce a falling toddler. A forehead's length from the unbarricaded stairs. We needed to renovate before she got her hands and knees in concert. We needed rubber and nets. I had so many things to see for her. So many edges. How would listening ever do?

Tess drank water from her sippy cup, then sputtered, then went quiet, perhaps breathing, perhaps not. My body lit up.

"Normal," Tracy pre-empted. "Relax."

I was a baby cough shy of a seizure.

"I can't relax," I said. "I'm hearing everything wrong."

Maybe I'd be better off eating in the next room, at least until she had teeth, or could use a knife and fork, or do her own taxes.

"You still hungry?" Tracy said to the baby. Several mmm's resonated from Tess's mouth. "Let's have Cheerios!"

"Please, no."

Cheerio? Isn't that what we say to someone who's going away, maybe for good? Might as well feed her bullets. I wanted to dig Tess's spoon into both my ears. A handful of cereal hit Tess's tray, and I prepared for the worst.

"Maybe we should give her just one at a time," I said.

"She's faster than that. C'mon."

"Okay, two."

"Mmm," Tess mumbled. Then, with more urgency, "*mmm.*"

This was the "Hurry up" version of her phrase, as if to remind me that her hunger and ability to eat far surpassed my ability to deliver one Cheerio at a time, to cope with my anxiety, or to monitor the safe, moistened demise of cereal. Then I heard Tracy whacking Tess on the back. Hard. Tess sputtered and up came a Cheerio. The last of my available adrenaline blew my eardrums.

"Aw, Jesus!" I slammed my face on the table and knit my hands over my head. "That's it, I CAN'T DO THIS," I said.

Tracy wasn't having any of it. "Oh, please," she said. "She's fine."

"I'm not. I can't listen to this."

"She's just learning how to chew. And you're learning what it sounds like. Be patient."

During that long summer of sputters and coughs, I sometimes missed the most obvious fact of our world: Tracy always watched, ready to pick up anywhere my body left off. She was so present and part of the mediation between me and my daughter that I sometimes couldn't see it. Or her. When Tracy and I are at our symbiotic best, she is invisible. It's the downside of her accomplishment as a sighted partner. She disappears and lets me grow within a supervised, but unobtrusive, independence. Tess wasn't the only one Tracy was teaching around here.

It's hard, though, to feel like a father, when you are also in need of so much instruction. Of so much parenting from your lover.

I have always struggled to live my blindness by a definition that keeps me from getting too mawkish or crazed, or worse. The most common pathology is to become mystical and romantic about the loss of sight. Oh, how beautiful and alive the world must seem to your other senses, some folks swoon. Sadly, smog is smog. I bet you really, really listen in a deeper way to your wife, some women say, and drift off into a fantasy of true exchange with their TV-loving husbands. I'd like to think so. Yes, I listen carefully to Tracy. Most of the time, however, she finds herself reciting the contents of my mail, or describing the precise whereabouts of my shoes. No mysticism or romance in any of that.

So for my money, I understand blindness as two specific problems, and only two: a glitch in mobility, and a difficulty interfacing with visual information, such as print. Everything else flows from those two sources. In that respect, supervising Tess was actually not about watching or not-watching, not about having too much sound overwhelming the picture, or about me learning how to feel her swallow without bugging her. This was about literacy. Tracy was right. I was learning how to listen to Tess, how to read her, and Tracy would be our translator until I knew what sounds I could expect, in what order and to what degree. I needed a range of tonal familiarity before I could hear deviations. All parents go through this to a degree. Mine was just amplified.

Until that literacy came about, Tracy would be my other baby monitor. A soft and patient technology.

A few weeks after my choking fixation, I came home with Tess from a walk, which had also at one time seemed to be an overwhelming danger, but now, like eating, had tempered itself into something I felt was as easy and old-hat as a walk should be. As routine as chewing.

Tracy was upstairs. Tess and I sat down on the couch and undertook the arduous procedure of removing her from the baby carrier and peeling off her layers of clothing and weatherproofing. Off came her hat and sweater and boots. Off came mittens and baby sunglasses. Tess protested the indignity that comes of having a blind man fumble his way through these things. I heard that much.

Then I smelled it. The house was on fire. Our house, not the one next door.

Seemed like something in the next room, in the kitchen, which would be the most likely source. I scooped Tess and pinballed my way to the stove. The smell dissipated. It grew stronger as we scurried back to the living room. I yarded furniture away from plug outlets. No waft of smoke there. I cleared things from the coffee table. Magazines and mail. Nothing felt hot. I called to Tracy, uncertain where to move with Tess, and groped for her clothes. I grabbed them from the coffee table. We'd make a getaway. I still had the carrier on. I shouted to Tracy for help, and declared the presence of fire.

Tracy bounded down the stairs, calling, "What?! What?!"

"There's a fire! I can smell it!"

Just as I was about to dress the baby, Tracy grabbed Tess's hat and sweater from my hands. She beat them on the table. They were on fire. They were the fire. Apparently I'd tossed them down on a candle and, you know, spread the warmth. You'd think I could've felt the heat, but holding a burning sweater is not unlike holding a match. You'll smell it long before you'll feel its presence near your skin.

When the crisis was over, Tess's clothes sported large, scorched holes. Her shoes had brown, burnt patches where the flames had licked. Otherwise everything was fine. No harm done, no foul to anything but baby fashion. Fire, like choking, is a very quiet danger.

"She's all right," I said to Tracy. "Lesson learned. Papa won't throw clothes around."

Tracy didn't seem relieved by my quick study. Though she helps in so many respects, she can't always anticipate everything, and suffers the consequences if she lets up her guard. It's tiring, I bet. She can't just enjoy a stupid candle. Got to do the forensics. Ryan might put clothes on this. Or the baby.

"You know what?" I said. "We should dress her in these and put a picture up on the blog. Let people speculate. What do you think?"

Tracy didn't make a sound. I heard her loud and clear.

The Extraordinary Times of Dick and Jane, and Spot

• • •

Our cranky pug, Cairo, is tan-coloured, or what the pug-crazed call "smutty apricot." We've had her for nearly a decade and, to answer your question, no, Cairo is about as far from a guide dog as an eyeless cat. That's not to imply, however, that I'm in control. She's a tractor that tows me into holly bushes, or impales me on fire hydrants. Given the priority shift from Cairo to Tess, I'm sure my castration has been our dog's goal.

During Tess's first six months, as she grew and her cognitive architecture developed, Cairo remained of no interest to our daughter. The pug, likewise, showed a deficit of affection for Tess. The pug treated Tess like some bald strumpet who'd poached our love. Now we occupied our hands with soothers and teething rings, not liver treats or Cairo's stinky velvet frog, her favourite summer chew toy. I didn't know dogs could discern betrayal.

Cairo even shot accompanying looks. Say what you will about anthropomorphizing pets, but pugs have expressive, furrowed brows and an awful lot of passive aggression. They are a subtle, thespian breed that can cock their heads and communicate the precise ennui and hurt of "Oh, why do you treat me so?"

That withering look, and Cairo's greatest indignation, was visited upon us when we made our attempt to initiate a bond between her and the baby. The plan was to place one of Tess's blankets under Cairo's dish, thereby associating the baby's smell with that doggy elixir, kibble. But Cairo wasn't having any of it. Our transparency was an insult. Cairo just gobbled her supper, ignored the blanket, glowered at Tess, and, if anything, accepted the blanket's smell as permission to eat the smell's creator.

We just kept the baby out of reach.

My preferred spot was at the kitchen table. Tess would sit upright on my knee, usually shaking a rattle with one hand and gnawing the other. All the sleep deprivation and crying aside—hers and ours—I relished this stage. Contained in my lap and engaged enough by such miracles as her fingers, my pocket lint or a wad of Saran Wrap, Tess would let me feel her movements and discoveries. She made fascinating new motions, new manipulations of objects, and, my God, the sounds. So many sounds. A rhythm might stumble from her rattle, then repeat once or twice while she blew raspberries, then Tess was on to the next thing, be it a pill bottle of dried beans, or a selection of Tupperware filled with rice or coins or buttons, or combinations for different acoustic effect. She could shake crap for hours. It may sound dull as dust balls, but Tom Waits could have cut percussion tracks around here. Our kitchen had so many different—uh—kitchen items.

Terrific thing was, from the shifting weight on my knee, and from her little body squirming in my hands, no matter what Tess was up to I could track the turn of her head and posture, follow her attention, and aim a kiss, or a tickle. Whatever seemed like baby fun. Holding Tess gave me a view, and I was more than happy to watch, as it were. My lap was the world. It was world enough, too, until something strange happened, and it was over.

Tess discovered Cairo.

Some might say it was inevitable. Some might argue that, sooner or later, Tess had to see something of interest, something other than myself and Tracy. But that's just loser talk. I should have fought harder to keep her on my lap, and her abilities on par with my own.

Put it this way. Remember that country ditty, "Mama Don't Let Your Babies Grow Up to Be Cowboys"? Now, catchiness aside, it's asinine child-rearing advice. Who wouldn't want a cowboy in the family? Neat hats in the closet, steaks in the freezer. What's the problem? My rewrite would lift in song the real heartache of developing infants, and go something like, "Mama, don't let your babies grow up to see dogs or Dora the Explorer or dolls or anything out there that might upstage your love." I'm telling you, that's a song with some truth and hurtin' in it. How could I compete with smutty apricot? I've got a dog from the pornographic spectrum of the rainbow. Who wouldn't look?

The terrible day in question, I heard the click of Cairo's paws approaching us from the left. Tess's head bobbed towards the sound. Cairo's clicking continued our way, then it passed behind my chair. But before Cairo emerged on the other side, Tess pivoted in anticipation. She'd not only observed Cairo coming, and tracked the moving dog, which was its own profound shift in perception, but she'd anticipated where Cairo was going, where an object in space would arrive if she watched and waited. Up until that moment she'd only experienced the visual world as a series of disconnected still images. Now, not only did she see something, and see motion, but she'd imagined the future in her own infant way, and she'd had mind enough to tell herself that tiny, tiny narrative about where the dog had been, and from that infer where it might be next. In seeing, she'd made her first story. Papa's little auteur.

Tracy was busy at the sink, but witnessed this new Tess arrive as well.

"Did you catch that? She's never done that before," Tracy said. "She just, like, watched the dog."

"Good seeing, punkin!" I cheered, and patted Tess's back, adding like a proud father after his child's first limping tuba solo, "Top shelf, punkin! Papa can't even do that."

I really was in awe, and I really was thrilled, and, at the same time, I was somewhat lost. Like Tess, something morphed in my cognition.

When Tess saw motion for the first time, I became part of a new scale. The one I'd grown accustomed to was gone, and so I felt dislocated. Papa vertigo.

I mean, here I was, at the kitchen table. Here I was, whatever that meant, but how did I get here? My past had telescoped me all this way. Such distance brings a lot with it. Part of me was still the teenager who'd survived more than a dozen car accidents, and an equal number of jousting matches with forklifts, and here I was, somehow the same person, only I was also the guy who'd been stalked by a man claiming Peter Jackson criminally implanted a microchip in his retina, and that I was the only one who could tell the world. (He should now consider it done.) But somewhere in me I also carried the younger blind man I could never be again, one who'd convinced a band of drunken Russian sailors that, despite my shaved head, I was not an American GI living in South Korea, and that I had no intention of jumping them, or of joining them in a search for somebody else to jump, or for anybody, as they put it, to "fuck fuck." I could tell you some stories. I've been lost on a mountain in Utah until I was found by a Czech woman in an SUV that pulsed with mariachi. I've been guided by a man in a bear costume, and by a drug dealer through his New York turf. So many ways I've been lost and found in this blind man's life. These, my stories, have always located me, and that's why I tell them. That's why we tell them, to know who we are, here.

And now, here I was, the guy whose baby saw the dog.

That was my new story. From it I felt that old burn of how significant and compelling it seemed, but also the halting frustration of how, at the same time, it was so bloody small. Baby-sized. I hadn't read a tale like this one since elementary school, when Dick saw Jane. Dick and Jane see Spot. Run, Spot, run. Ironically, only as a father did I finally understand what that book is really about. Big, big stuff, actually. Tess sees. Tess sees Cairo. Run, Cairo, run.

The story is a humble one. It's also profound with transformation, and so unlike life before Tess. Maybe this profound minimalism was the new scale of our lives, and a measure of the new me. Babypapa.

Without question Tess was getting bigger and more complicated every day. But she was also growing her story. Growing a life that acquires its own description. Babies have only a handful of verbs. They eat, shit, cry, spit up, sleep, smile and wiggle. As a new parent, you live inside those few verbs with your child for the first year. In a sense, that's part of the disorientation on top of sleep deprivation and all the other usual suspects. Some mornings I'd catch myself sitting with Tess and shaking the rattle, as I had the day before, and the day before that, or listening to her cry, or to her feed, and wonder where the hell all my verbs had gone. The baby ate my verbs. Could somebody open a window in here?

This might ultimately explain why parents are so punishing with their anecdotes. We are ecstatic, as if thawed from a long, cryogenic sleep, with each rejuvenating action taken by our kids, no matter how banal. Like tourists with too many holiday slides, we prattle on to bored strangers, celebrating our return from new frontiers. "My God," we say, "you should have seen the baby and the thing he did with the garden hose the other day! And this morning he made a brand new sound, sort of like he said 'multifaceted' but, thing is, we don't even use that word around the house, do we, hon!" Parents—all of us—send dispatches from another dimension where babies watching dogs, or futzing with garden hoses, is something blockbuster. And it is. Like, wow.

Or maybe you just had to be there.

Meanwhile, back in the kitchen, the story carried on. Tess giggled at the dog, Cairo still unaware of her new celebrity status as the third living thing in Tess's world.

Stories like this one happened almost every day. We'd witnessed all sorts of changes, most of them involving the discovery of motor control, or aim, or the exercise of force, things of that nature, and every time a new skill manifested, Tracy and I were struck by how astonishing such rudimentary talents really are. When was the last time I stumbled into something my body could do? More than that, did it change my relationship to reality? Nothing comes to mind.

I could be faced with such a transformation one day. Say I had my sight restored. Genetic engineering is closing in on both a prevention platform for RP and a restorative therapy. Of course I say groovy to that, and let's buy stock. But I also have to ask what a cure would mean. Certainly I'd finally see Tess, and I'd likewise see the dog walk across the kitchen for the first time in years, but I also wouldn't know who I was any more, or how to proceed. To comprehend and manage constant visual input, like its obverse, blindness, would be another trauma altogether. Like body-switching. Just to imagine, then, Tess's discovery of her hands. Or, to imagine those first fluid moving pictures of consciousness, and the dog that walked from here to there. Hoo boy. No wonder babies need a nap.

Not long after that, Tess began to point, mostly at the smutty apricot thing, then to other things, then to pretty much every object in the house. My new job as a father, as if Tess had learned it from watching Cairo, was to fetch stuff, and to make it come closer to her drooling mouth. It wasn't easy. Because of our new pastime, I often felt like Master Blaster, that creature from the third *Mad Max* film, the one with Tina Turner and the Thunderdome. In case you missed it—lucky you—Master Blaster consisted of one idiot-man, Blaster, the mute, soft-brained giant who carried another man on his back, Master, who was a scheming dwarfy fellow who bossed Blaster about, sort of like a rider to a pack mule. Or Tess to her Papa.

"Dat, dat," she'd insist, and jab, jab her index finger in the air, aiming us, sort of.

Little did Tess know that such pointy-words mean nothing to me, be it this, that, there or them. Pointy fingers mean even less, their shape and direction obliterated by the fluid in my retinas. Undeterred, Tess continued to point, even when sitting on my knee, the way we used to. But now she was frustrated and bored. Our contained utopian playground wasn't enough any more. She'd already outgrown my lap, and was heading beyond my ability to track. She was becoming sighted, and that left me behind in the blindness that she didn't understand. Language would change that. But when would it come? When would it bridge us?

Here I was, and there she went. Tess was learning what was out "there," while I was stuck in here, the place where she'd once been blind and content, too. It was my turn to grow and change. Somehow I had to catch up.

See Papa run. Run, Papa, run.

ACT THREE

. . .

Given to Words

Lost in Space

• • •

Once babies discover how to track things in motion, the next big, hard, ugly lesson is that those moveable objects can disappear. When a beloved person passes through a door, say, she vanishes. Poof. It isn't clear, however, that the vanished can and will come back, morbid exceptions aside.

The first time I took care of Tess on my own was Mother's Day. Yes, Mother's Day. The name should have been a clue. Our success at walks around the block had been enough to buoy my confidence, and Tracy's. I was ready. I could do this. Tracy could now comfortably indulge in a well-deserved break for, my God, an hour. Maybe more. Maybe slightly over an hour.

The window of responsibility may sound small, a skimpy treat for Tracy who really carried the bulk of Tess's waking day. Absolutely. No argument from me, and I wished Tracy could take more time for herself. But, then again, close your eyes and tend to a newborn for an hour. You'll count the minutes, too, as will the baby's mother.

I bought Tracy a visit to a downtown day spa. There she'd retreat into some well-deserved pampering, calm and quiet. Meanwhile, Tess would dangle from the Bjorn while I lugged her about the area, Master Blaster taking in the city sights. Likely, though, Tess would just pass out and drool. Her own spa experience, as it were.

The adventure began, as always, with Tess crying in the car, all the way to the spa, then amping-up when we loaded her onto my chest. She wanted her mom. I, of course, was not her mom. Worse, Tess could now see that I was the giant, idiot-man to whom she was strapped. Days prior I'd been her celebrated private carriage and gofer, but now I was a torture mechanism that kept her at a forced remove from the soft, perfumy comfort of Tracy's arms.

Such are a baby's perceptions. I simply reassured myself that her despondence would pass as soon as she saw something new and of interest, such as, well, who knows. Anything was possible. A mailbox or burger wrapper, maybe a window display of men's shoes. Maybe we'd wander into a tattoo parlour and examine the blood and grimaces. Tracy did her best to calm Tess outside the spa, then smiled and cooed just one last time before taking off. Her tone was reluctant, however, and already somewhat dispirited. It saddened me. It implied Tracy knew all too well that we'd eventually have to follow her inside and cut her time short. Tracy felt strapped to Tess in a different way.

"Have fun, sweetie," she instructed the baby, or me, then disappeared into the spa, leaving us on the sidewalk.

"See?" I said, "Mommy's gone in there for—"

A mushroom cloud went off in the Bjorn.

"No, no! Mommy's just gone inside for a minute. She'll be back!"

Tracy could hear Tess raging on the other side of the glass. The spa people could, too. They swarmed Tracy, identifying her as the mother who needed emergency measures of aromatherapy and massage, given the wailing outside, and the panicking blind man she'd left to fix it.

Reflexively I knew the first task was to distract. Get a hook in Tess, then sustain a steady flow of stimulation, all manner of fun and wizardry, so that at no time would there be lapse enough to think, "Hey, where's mom, is she—oh, wait, mom's still ALWAYS NEVER COMING BACK FOREVER!"

But I can admit I've never been a good babysitter. While technically this was not babysitting, Tess being my own flesh and adoration, my skill set for the situation hadn't been exercised since my teens, when I could see, and even then as a babysitter I had no idea what to do with the kids other than have them watch me watch music videos, watch me empty the house of chips, and then watch me send them to bed early. Really early.

Don't get me wrong. We'd had some fun, too. Or at least what I thought was fun. It helped that the neighbours who'd hired my pimply presence were a spectacularly religious family. On Halloween they were the ones who gave out handmade brochures that featured a colourful bullet-point list of steps to salvation. They were a nice enough family, and asked that I simply provide some good, clean activities for their two girls one evening, while the parents pursued something redemptive, but adult-oriented, on their own. No problem.

After I'd jacked up on relatively meagre junk food rations, and after I'd exposed the girls to enough Skinny Puppy videos to guarantee nightmares, we finished the day by making up new prayers at bedtime. That was around, I dunno, six o'clock or so.

I knelt with them by their beds, and led the two girls in recitation.

"Our father, Art in heaven—"

"No, no," the oldest girl snapped. "It's 'Our father, WHO art in heaven,' dummy."

"Really? I don't think so."

"Is too so!" she said.

"But I'm older than you, so you're wrong."

"And you're a dummy dumbhead."

She was eight years old, and already destined to be a workplace harassment officer.

"That may be," I said, "but it's just 'Our father, Art in heaven.' God's name is Art. And where does Art live? He lives in Heaven."

The littlest girl's jaw dropped. I'd just peeled back the veil of reality to show its first secret name.

"God's name is Art?" she said.

"Yes. In fact he has many names."

"Like what names?"

"Let's see," I said, and continued the prayer. "Our father, Art in Heaven, Howard be thy name."

"Stop it!" the harassment officer cried. "You're not supposed to say that."

"I can't say Howard?"

I was never invited back.

Tess was too young for an improvised exegesis of the

Lord's Prayer, so I just walked. The motion of a brisk pace was usually enough to calm her, and that may have remained true, but I was immediately confronted with an unanticipated obstacle.

I had no idea where we were.

I didn't know this area of town. Specifically, I had no idea what was around me, and what was the safest direction to explore. More pressing still, where did the stairs go? I knew we'd initially climbed some stairs from where we'd parked, yet it seemed we'd remained on a sidewalk after that, as we walked to the spa's storefront window. A sidewalk in the sky. Tess was already damp with tears. Howard had it in for me.

We turned away from the door, the one that had eaten Tess's mom, and poked about, caning for the edge. Tess's new spatial understanding of where we were, and how to go, was probably more informed than mine. Few visual clues were available. Though good light was shining, and my face was warmed as I shuffled towards it, its painful brightness also bleached away any smears that my eyes might offer. When Tess screamed louder, I assumed the sun was also in her eyes, so we turned and inched along the lip of our abyss. My sense of space was so malnourished that I felt we were on a tightrope, when, for all I knew, we may have actually been standing in the middle of a wide, empty pedestrian boulevard.

Tess eulogized her mother. Unable to find the stairs, I could only hope I wouldn't make our day an audition for *Thelma & Louise.* Each safely planted foot became a victory, and a significant expansion of the known universe. My ears were frantic and searched for any signs of traffic under the baby's protests. I wasn't so concerned we'd be pulverized—last I saw, cars don't climb stairs—but mostly I wanted their orientation. Where there's traffic, there's direction. Same with stairs and hallways or doorways. Blind folks, like infants, love to be confined. It tells us where we are. At that moment I would have gladly taken up residency in a crib.

Dozens of zigs and zags later we found an intersection, but no stairs. Somehow sky had collapsed to street level but without decline, or ramp, or escalator. I turned us around and retraced our steps. I've learned to make only the shortest forays into the unknown before checking my ability to recreate the path. It's nothing as tidy or productive as two steps forward, one step back. That would be zippy. Sadly, a walk with me goes something more like one hundred steps forward, one hundred and ten back, two hundred forward, one-forty back, look lost, wait for help. I hate going for a walk.

Toddlers do the same thing. They run away from their parents, then boomerang back, and not just out of love or fear of retribution, but as a necessary brain exercise. At this stage, the kiddies are actually learning how to map their way back—how to imagine space, and their passage through it—and so the most disorienting thing a parent can do is give chase. For the kid, it must be like, "Hey, how the hell did you get here when I just broke a sweat trying to get away from you? Let's try that again." And they're off.

Toddler and blind man similarities end there. My fantasy existence involves a twenty-four-hour concierge who tails me every step of the way.

My feet picked up pace and headed up the street to amuse Tess with the sights of, of, what?

When calm and engaged, the baby could do her best to point Master Blaster in the direction of her curiosity, but now I was immersed in the other half of that problem: I couldn't offer her much of the world beyond. As we walked, I tried to point to things and give them names, trying to bring her the city, but I was faced with just how atrophied my picture of the city, as toggled by its sounds and smells, really is.

"Look, punkin," I said, "look at the big, uh, building."

A safe guess, I figured.

We shuffled some more and I searched my senses for something else to show her.

"And look over there," I said, waving my hand ambiguously, "there's another building, see?"

The wailing continued. She was not interested, and I couldn't blame her. Might as well entertain ourselves with a series of squares called "stuff."

We shuffled further down the block, until I clipped my hip against something cold, metallic and rigid. Cities have many of these. It didn't budge, but I sure did, and the surprise force just about dumped us on our collective back. Tess let me know she was not a fan of slapstick.

"Hey, look," I said, and pointed to the cold, metallic thing. "It's, uh, metal, this thing. And it's, like, cold. Let's call it a bike rack. Unless it isn't. "

I bounced her and faced the passing traffic, my only other certainty.

"Hear the cars? Maybe there's a truck out there. Do you see, uh, a vehicle?"

Recently the problem had manifested in another way. Tracy had walked into Tess's room one afternoon to find us reading a book in the Big Song Chair.

"You're holding the book upside down," Tracy said as she put away some baby laundry.

I up-ended the book, turned the page and continued, "The people on the bus go up and down, up and—"

Tracy interrupted. "You've got *Walter the Farting Dog*, not *Wheels on the Bus*."

"Oh, right."

Now the book felt thick and empty. I continued to stare at the colourful smudges, ready to read, but nothing came to mind. My disdain for Braille dissolved.

"Uh, how does this go?" I finally asked Tracy.

"It's called *Trouble at the Yard Sale.* The father sells the farting dog to a clown. There's a bank robbery in the end with balloons."

"Right. Okay. Here we go, punkin. One day there was a farting dog. There was a yard sale, too, and this clown, see, this clown came along and—"

I'd memorized the handful of animals that populated *Peek-a-Moo,* and I could recall the single phrase on each page of *Brown Bear, Brown Bear, What Do You See?* and I'd even fudged the connective tissue to recite an approximation of Three Little Pigs, but now I blanked. What the hell connects a farting dog at a yard sale to a robbery with a clown? I didn't want Tess to think buses are dogs, and farts are whatever Papa made up that day when he pretended to show her the picture book.

So I just turned the pages and began a half hour of, "Wow" and "Look at that big, uh, colour."

Out here in the city, I felt that same deep parental craving to teach Tess, and to give her the proper names, but too few connections were available. The story had an infinitely small vocabulary.

Then I heard it. A pop and buzz in the distance, maybe down the next block or so. Construction. Lots of noises, lots of accurate pictures in my mind. Bonus. If Tess's crying persisted, I could muffle it under the jackhammers. Meanwhile, I could say, "Look, a jackhammer!" We hurried towards the noise.

As we neared the construction Tess stopped crying and began to giggle. Hammers banged, saws buzzed and a backhoe dug. I had a palette of nouns and verbs and all sorts of pointing to do. She squealed and wriggled in the Bjorn, and I relaxed, confident with what to say, and where we were. Of the time since Tess had arrived in our lives, these few minutes felt among the warmest I'd spent, and intimated what raising a child could fundamentally mean. I was teaching. I was discerning for her. Making the world bigger with each word, each name taking another step further from the blur and haze, and into our human specificity. Tess was in awe, and I had the names for that awe. I could then stick them to the world with the tip of my index finger. God, it was fantastic. I highly recommend it.

My ears scanned. More construction down the street. When we exhausted that visit, I tracked more for us down another block or so. Every time we approached the safety fence of another construction pit, Tess giggled and I named what she saw. No more crying, we hopscotched about town for nearly an hour this way until, finally, she'd had enough.

But enough is a bit of an understatement. Recharged by the energy of dump trucks and cranes and crashing metal, as well as the bright sun and its heat, Tess was overstimulated. She mustered, let's just say, an unprecedented expression of despair. She wanted her mom, and nower than now.

"Don't worry, punkin," I said. "Let's go back. We'll find Mommy. We'll go fast."

I turned on my heel and surveyed my mental map of the streets for the fastest route back.

That would first require knowing where we were.

We'd lily-padded site to site and I hadn't kept track of our movements. Construction sites echoed in several directions. My breadcrumbs were gone.

I banged my cane and hurried as best I could, this way, then that. Each block sounded the same as the next, so back and forth I paced, unable to commit to a direction, struggling to remember where we'd been, the sequence of turns my body had made, and the rough measure of time that had passed between each of those turns. When you're blind, however, it's almost impossible to reconstruct such a map while you're busy walking, which forces your brain to archive a new map simultaneously. Hell is an eternity of multitasking. The perils of signposts and sandwich boards had to be dealt with, too. All the while Tess screamed and writhed, as if I'd stolen her from her real family, and yet nobody, not a single phantom silhouette, stopped us or asked if we needed help.

Could I blame them? Not really. Stop and ask a blind guy and his upset baby if they're lost, you may end up stuck with them on your elbow until Wisconsin.

Tess needed immediate comfort, or tending of some kind. One last pause, then I committed us to a regrettable action. In mid-search I undid the Bjorn and took her out. For good. Remember, I can't wrap a diaper on a good day, let alone reinsert an aggravated baby into a harness.

Vacating the Bjorn sure pissed her off. Both my hands went to work, feeling if anything was wrong—something pinching her, a full diaper, any puke slick or Braille-like evidence of a rash or something. Anything—but nothing revealed itself.

Just your average baby meltdown, it seemed. To all appearances she was fine, unlike the blind man, who now needed two hands to carry the screaming baby, and a third to cane. The latter activity would have to go. I tucked my stick under my arm and went kamikaze.

Yes, no cane.

Who knew anything could be slower than my normal pace? At that moment I invented a unique style of microstepping. If we could have moved any slower, time would have reversed and brought us back to the spa by quantum physics. Onward we shuffled, Tess cradled to my shoulder, my cane pinched under my arm. Buses and trucks blew by. Bikes grazed my elbows as they rocketed past. The danger was heightened by the fact nobody recognized me as blind any more. A folded cane doesn't signify well. So far we'd made it less than one block of our enormous return.

A few of the passing footsteps were attached to voices, and one of those voices was finally kind enough to give me directions to the spa.

"It's over that way," a man's voice said.

"There?" I pointed.

He grabbed my index finger and swung it around in the opposite direction.

"There, that way," he said. "So, you're going for a spa, eh? Sounds like your baby could use one."

I think he laughed at his own joke, but I couldn't hear much over Tess, what with her esophagus swallowing my ear.

"And how far do I go?" I asked.

"You wanna cross the street. Boy, he's sure fussy, ain't he?"

"Yeah, right, fussy. And where do I go after that?"

"Uh, the spa, I guess. It's just over there."

"It's just across the street?"

"You didn't know that?"

About eighteen thousand caneless steps later we were in the zone, albeit down with the cars, not up on our sidewalk in the sky. Tess's cries echoed off the concrete wall we needed to ascend.

"See this, punkin," I said, "this is what they call a fucking hard time. See? And see that wall? That's a fucking nightmare."

I had a great number of things for Tess that I could accurately name—my cane was fucking useless, my eyes were fucking broken, my arms were fucking sore and I was an example of someone far from fucking capable of life beyond his neighbourhood.

Then I listened. I mean, I really listened, and in listening I realized what I was doing wrong. I wasn't paying attention to Tess.

We scurried along the wall, in front of the parked cars, and made another pass at the block. This time, however, I stopped every ten paces or so, and held Tess out so she, and her wailing desperation, squarely faced the wall. Her cries echoed back every time, until, about mid-block, I heard a difference. A lesser resolve in her tone. Her voice travelled up the empty stairwell and pointed the way.

Together we'd engineered infant sonar.

The first thing I did when we reached the home stretch of glass storefronts was threaten a window with my cane. Nothing brings help like that. A bell tinkled as a door shot open nearby.

"Wait! Are you looking for your wife?" a breathless woman asked.

"My God, yes, please."

I shimmied into the spa, clueless where to go. I could tell the space was large and modern, sleek and spare, as Tess's voice ricocheted about, filling the rooms. It must have jarred all those napping mothers. I didn't have to ask where to find Tracy.

"Shall I take the baby," the woman said, "uh, for you?"

"My God, please," I said.

Tess's voice diminished into the distance. She was carried away, and down a hall, and into a room. By the time I caught up, she was nuzzled to her mom, calmed and nursing.

"Was she like this the whole time?" Tracy asked.

"Naw, not at all," I said. "How was your massage?"

"Fantastic. We're almost done."

An awkwardness hung in the air.

"Almost?" I checked.

"Yeah. About fifteen minutes left."

"Right. Okay," I said. "I suppose I can always just take her outside for a little walk or something."

My Dad Went to Kansas City and All i Got Was this Stupid Button

• • •

In the pinch of a coffee break some moms tear across town and nurse their eight-week-old infants at an overcrowded daycare. Then they have to elbow their way back to work before somebody gets pissy and sabre-rattles about the virtues of baby formula. Usually that particular somebody is concerned because he has a moustache and no kids of his own. Not that he knows of.

Or there are spreadsheets. These are schedules distributed to extended family and vaguely familiar neighbours in order to enlist childcare. Some report a feeling of relief once such a system is in place. Right. Then, a week later, parents actually find themselves in a suspended state of guilt about abandoning their baby before he can say, "Daddy-who?" Good times.

It seems to be one of the above situations, or somebody stays home and the bills pile up twice as fast with only one paycheque. I could go on but I won't, since we suffered none of it.

You may be wondering why, in writing about a first year of fatherhood, both Tracy and I are at home together pretty much all the time. We were. Who's working, you ask? How did this utopia come about and what catalogue did we order it from?

When Tess was born, the college offered me a year-long paternity leave. They said they would keep my salary in place for a couple of semesters while I stayed home. I know, I know. Don't punch me. Tracy's employer only offered, well, nothing. Just whatever the government minimum guaranteed, which was far less than my hot-rod, topped-up paternity benefit. So, we had to choose. Only one parent at a time is covered, but the fact we got to choose is worth a cheer. According to my employer, a father can be the primary caregiver, and should suffer no financial penalty for taking on that responsibility. How liberal and progressive. How cool is that?

Thing is, I couldn't be the primary caregiver. If I'd tried, we might not have had our little girl for long. Sure, I could have called Tracy at work and asked for help, but how would she know where I put the soother, or the bottle. Or our child? Questions such as, "Is she all right?" or, "Where did Tess put her diaper?" are hard to answer over the phone. Tracy would have died of nervous exhaustion.

Even a social worker agreed we'd have had problems. A few months after Tess was born, I met one at the coffee shop. She was on her rounds. Twice a week she visited a blind single mom in the neighbourhood. The purpose was to ensure that the child was healthy, clean, fed and so on. Cared for, in other words. As she stirred a latte, the social worker casually asked if I had anybody coming by the house, or, you know, if I'd considered a visit? The question seemed presumptuous. Invasive, even. My morning coffee had become a sales pitch for government intervention.

The offer hurt at first. But then I realized what the social worker was looking at. Tess was hanging on my chest, and I hadn't noticed the snot running down her face, nor the soother she'd abandoned by the door, beside her shoe.

Ultimately Tracy and I decided we would both spend the year at home, even though our house would sorely miss Tracy's income. No biggy. I had a plan. The theory was simple, as all good plans should be: to make some extra cash, I would lock myself in the basement beside the washing machine—which scrubbed various body fluids from our clothes at all hours—and there I would write from six in the morning till noon. After that I could join the girls upstairs, or spell off Tracy. Our dreamy family dynamic. A writer and a dad, together at last.

I enjoy a good delusion.

At some hazy point after Tess arrived, the architecture of our house changed. Nobody told us this would happen. I'd assumed when I went to work in the basement that there would remain a distinction between upstairs and downstairs. Nuh uh. Tess and her needs, noises and displays were in fact ubiquitous. I might take my post, poised over the keyboard, then hear Tess fuss or sneeze two floors above, and be compelled to investigate. Worse, Tracy might laugh at some Tess shenanigans, and I'd know I was missing something critical. Up and down I went, unable to focus or finish a sentence, let alone a Tess-less thought. To have assumed, then, that I could merely retreat somewhere else in the house to write had been thoroughly naïve on my part. As was my other assumption. I'd also assumed I could write.

Let's just say I could type. That might even be too generous.

I could depress keys, but banging my head against the keyboard would have been more communicative, and a better use of my head. My mind was everywhere but here, beside the washing machine, where I needed it to earn that extra income and keep us home. I really wanted to write, too. The compulsion felt stronger than ever. It even had an extra biological drive. When Tracy would sit down to breastfeed, my hands felt itchy and purposeless. I'd dog her with questions. Can I get you something? The lighting okay? Pillow? What do you need? If those didn't work, I'd volley my real desperation—What do *I* do?

Yes, that's the phrase you hear way off in the distance, late at night. It is the howl of the new fathers.

When breast feeding, Tracy's, er, direct contribution to Tess only illuminated my lack of purpose, so I wanted to do something. Write. Bring home bacon, be resourceful and necessary. Half of the household equation. The other challenge, of course, is that a father can seem to be running away from responsibility when in fact he just wants to do stuff, and then do more of it, because there are a lot of verbs that need tending to. Writing was one of mine.

But I just stared at the blurry light of my laptop. Where in my head had the ticker-tape of sentences gone? My career was over. Where had it gone? Then the cause of my problem snuck up on me in a fit of insight.

Tess ate my brain.

I tried to think of another cause. Nope. Couldn't. There you go, even further proof that I had no brain. It was true.

Writing is what finishes in your computer, but begins when you're everywhere else. An imagination exercises in the most unlikely moments: in the shower, while walking the dog, as you chew a steak, or in the liminal consciousness between waking and sleeping. Give me your shoe polish and I'll give you back a chapter. That's how the brain steals time for its work, so when you do finally sit down in the early, childless morning, lots of words and phrases and stories are piled up, ready to go, like kids with their faces pressed to the window, itchy for the recess bell to let them out.

Or that's how it's supposed to go. Then along comes a baby. Any time that had been given to my professional imagination was gone. What time remained had been colonized by baby thoughts and baby fun and baby needs. Wonderful stuff, a head full of sippy cups, but just as empty in other respects. Now I couldn't breastfeed, and I couldn't work, either. How to dispatch myself as a stay-at-home dad was shaping up to be more of a puzzle than I had anticipated. Despite it all, I made myself sit at my desk and write one word, then another, and eventually I did what any author does to confront writer's block. I Googled crap.

To grant the full illusion of genuine inquiry, I even Googled "dad" and "work" and "not." Well done, I thought. A smidgen of writing and a smidgen of research. At least Tracy heard some typing.

And that's how I discovered the consortium of North American stay-at-home dads online, including their blogs, chat forums, self-feeding circuit of hyperlinks and, most astonishing of all, an open invitation to their national convention in Missouri. The dads were about to get offline and get together for a few days of mano-a-mano time, and time to . . . do what exactly?

I reserved my hotel and booked a plane ticket to Kansas City. There I would meet my kin and, hopefully, find out what it is we at-home dads do, and how, and why. Or something. They hadn't posted a program online. Tracy wanted to know more about the plan, too.

"Well, all I know is we're going to have workshops on various topics," I explained.

"Such as?"

"Oh, the usual stuff. You know."

"No, I don't," she reminded me.

I was hard at work packing my suitcase, not unlike the way others pack a burrito. Jam shit inside, then quickly contain the situation.

"Oh, the workshops are just dad things," I said. "Why won't this close?"

"Dad things?"

Tracy handed Tess over, and began to refold my shirtwads. I sat on the edge of our bed and bounced Tess on my knee, unaware that she was trying to grab the bedside lamp. Tracy noticed.

"Careful," she panicked, "you've got her, she's almost—!"

"It's all right, I got her." I softened our bouncing. "Better?"

Tracy shoved the lamp aside. "You have no idea what you're going to do at this convention."

"Me? Well, no."

Tracy's mind, I imagine, was doing some writing of its own. Hers was composing the most likely workshop titles to be found at a Kansas City fathers' jamboree. These may have included, "Getting Loaded with Strangers," "How To Sleep in Like a Dad Who Got Loaded with Strangers," and "You and Your Room Service, Spa, Cable TV, Indoor Pool Issues."

But I was serious. I wanted to learn all manner of Daddy stuff, glean some techniques for now and for the long haul.

I would mine the wisdom of my peers, and maybe, just maybe, they could help me field some of the oncoming curve balls. The evidence suggests that all dads are, for example, temporarily blinded when styling their little girl's hair, right? Surely they had tips.

As I sealed my luggage burrito, Tracy imagined a scenario I'd dodged.

"What if they're into Robert Bly?" she threatened.

I thought about the Promise Keepers. This could be a front for patriarchal zealots. There could be chanting. Tracy put it another way.

"And what if," she said, "you end up in the woods, in a power circle and, you know . . ."

Not the drums. Anything but the drums.

" . . . and drumming," she finished.

That lit a fear.

"Well," she said, "I guess at least you'll have something to write about."

The majority of us arrived at the hotel late and sequestered ourselves away to sleep. A few didn't. They were the ones whose hands were clammy, and whose voices were pocked and raspy with hangover the next day.

Breakfast was a buffet meet-and-greet. Lots of high fives and fist-punching popped in the air. Most of the guys seemed to know each other from prior conventions, or from their various blogging identities. The atmosphere was festive, as if costumes had been removed. The stranger with the white cane stared at the blobs on the buffet table and wondered what they were, and if they were the breakfast, and if this was, indeed, the buffet table.

I lowered my fingers to investigate. They pierced a cluster

of scrambled eggs. A man offered to assemble a plate. What would I like? I'm not sure I even answered before a storm of dadness engulfed me. The man dispatched two of his friends to get coffee and juice, and another to fetch a plate. The large hand of another pressed a wad of napkins into my palm. Then I was steered to an already crowded table. At this rate they would wipe my nose, fix my bike and enroll me in Boy Scouts before I finished my bowl of cereal.

The orchestrator of my breakfast, Michael, was from Canada. He'd travelled all this way from the Quebec Eastern Townships. This was his fourth convention, though he'd been an at-home dad for nearly eight years. Michael and I were the only Canadians among the hundred or so participants. Another had attended the year before, but he'd disappeared from the online community, perhaps back to wage work, as they often explained any attrition.

I eavesdropped on others. The genre of introduction was unfamiliar. Nobody here greeted by profession, or quickened to it, as in, "So, Bob, what do you do?" Or, "Hey, Balthazar, how's fibreglass treating you?" Here people presented themselves by their number of children, and the number of years spent at home. Both numbers were reported with pride. These were pilots with their hours in the air, or vets with their tours of duty. Engines, NASA and baseball cards have statistics. So do dads.

Somebody reached across the table to shake my hand. I didn't notice, so he literally picked up my arm and rattled it. The gesture was brave and friendly. Too bad his fingers took away my breakfast grease.

"Hi, I'm Dave. From Wisconsin. Got two girls at home and a boy on the way. Your first convention?"

"Yep." I smiled. "Her name's Tess."

"How terrific is that! Got a picture?"

I barely had one in mind, let alone in my wallet or in the luggage burrito. In fact, I'd forgotten that sighted people carry pictures of their kids. What if somebody asked for proof? Showing up to a dad's convention without photos was like showing up to AA without guilt.

"Sorry," I said. "Blind guy thing. I forgot."

Dave quickly introduced me to a number of men from all over the US, with all numbers of children and years logged. Clark was from Texas and had four kids, and more than a decade at home. Before that he was a lawyer. Several other men were academics on hiatus. Their partners earned more money, or enjoyed more job security, and so these dads had opted to abandon wage work until their kids were ready for school. I began to feel like an imposter. I still worked at home. Was that illegal here? In my mind I clung to writer's block for legitimacy. More men introduced themselves. Surrounding me were truck drivers, house painters, office managers and bartenders. You had to dig to find out, but the entire employment spectrum seemed to be in our collective past.

With greetings done, and breakfast licked, we were ready to go—sort of. Official proceedings wouldn't begin until the next day. We arrived, in other words, to a day off. The immediate future was reserved for sight-seeing, shopping, and anything that didn't involve the word "potty."

You can imagine the problem this posed. How would Tracy, a single mom for the weekend, feel about my arrival to free time? Didn't I come here to learn how to cope with less? A token Kansas City BBQ apron wouldn't be enough. I already owed her for this time, now I owed even more.

"Say," Dave said as clusters of men began to disperse, "you wanna come with us?"

Alone in a strange city, I would either be flattened as I wandered the highway, or be bored to death by the safety of the hotel lobby. In either case, I wouldn't know how to find the potty. Washroom, I mean. Dave was my man.

An hour later we waited in a cavernous room, and were greeted by a woman who requested that we leave behind all our worldly possessions. "Security," she explained. Next we shuffled down a hall, into a tiny room, and assembled ourselves on benches in front of a screen, as if we were about to be recruited into military service. Maybe we'd take personality tests. Lights dimmed. An amphetamine-techno beat pulsed. The screen lit up and strobed, accelerating to match the fury of what sounded like a racing engine. A narrator intoned a lengthy menu of corporate success slogans. Though the room sounded like a training seminar for Japanese auto executives, the narrator welcomed us to, what else, Harley Davidson. Kansas City is where they build the bikes that roar down our streets and wake our babies.

As the company's corporate history unfolded on the screen, I sat on my bench and wondered what the hell we were doing here. Nostalgia? Did our tour guide understand that the parking lot was currently filled with minivans, and that those minivans were full of baby car seats? Behind me, in low tones, two men ignored the film and debated the virtues of slow-cookers. Both had good points.

Soon we toured around the factory floor, past a series of robots that measured, cut and welded gas tanks. These machines used to be people, and though we were encouraged to behold the razzle-dazzle of technology, I felt sad. Dispirited for the ghosts of welders. The air smelled of smoke. Sparks, snaps of electricity, and the hiss of acetylene all conjured memories of my father. He'd laboured nights as a welder through much of my childhood. This place smelled and sounded of him, and of his secret life on the graveyard shift.

How I loved the fact that my father worked graveyards. Even the word was dark and powerful, like him, and his job was all of that to me, too. You can imagine the thrill when I was allowed to visit him one night at the warehouse where he made chain link fences. A peek behind the veil. I remember how my hands swam inside his heavy leather gloves, and how his safety goggles swallowed my face. Far from embarrassed, I burned with pride to be placed inside his uniform. I went to work. Or, my little boy's idea of work.

For an hour I scavenged bits of wire from the grimy shop floor. Then I stacked them in bundles beside my dad's workbench. That's it. That was my first job. No, I wasn't cleaning the floor. I believed my father could put the wires back together. He could do anything. That's why the factory needed him.

There, in the Harley factory, something occurred to me. While I loved being at home with Tess, I realized, as I remembered the graveyard shift, that I equally loved the bond of work's mystery. I wanted to come home to Tess every day, and in doing so, intimate for her some great, wide world out there. My own father, in coming home from work, had seemed a giant. I'd felt as safe as he seemed capable and large in the world that he returned from.

But as a blind father, I felt I had so little security to give. Excusing myself from the duties of fatherhood was no solution, that much I knew. While it may have kept Tess safe, it didn't give her a fully realized dad, or a bond. I would have to earn that every day. Bring experience to her. Good and bad. It's the job.

That night we consolidated as a group in the hospitality suite. I don't remember much in the way of details, other than I was consistently thumped on the shoulder by the slaphappy. Such whacking mostly followed the statement, or question, "Jeez, so, like for serious, how do you change a diaper?"

These dads could immediately see the land mines ahead. What are you gonna do when she can run? You know she'll run, don't you? How will you know if she's opened a bottle of drain cleaner or something? How will you know where she is on the playground? I have two words for you, my man: potty training. Do you have a system? How do you know where the nearest john is in a mall? These guys knew the questions I had, but they didn't have any answers. I drank a lot of beer. One dad swore by the power of hockey pucks.

"My advice to you is to stack 'em in the freezer," he said. "I keep a half dozen in there at all times. Perfect for teething. Per-fect."

My face said I had misgivings.

"Sorry, no offence," he said.

My pinched expression was at the thought of Tess sucking on industrial rubber, not at my segregation from our most revered sport.

Nobody seemed to be in great shape the next day for our official start as we sat around small tables and quietly nursed our coffees, flipped through our conference packages, and tried to keep our Danishes down. My eyes felt like hard-boiled eggs, and, true to hardboiled eggs, they couldn't read my workshop schedule. Nor did I feel like asking anyone. Not to worry. I would let the day's proceedings surprise me.

Our official welcome began. As the plenary speaker took the stage, the worst thing possible actually happened.

We were asked to stand.

Nothing good ever comes of being asked to stand. That's especially true during a talk. I'd already done my thespian duty as a cervix. Nobody warned me that fatherhood propels you into a life of interactive role play with strangers. At that moment I could barely cope with gravity, never mind kick-off calisthenics or, far worse, an ice-breaker game. Go on, shake hands with three people to your left and introduce yourself in the character of your first pet.

But the speaker began with a different set of instructions.

"Gentlemen," he boomed, "for those of you who attended last year, this will be familiar. For those of you who are new, try to follow along and keep up. When I say eyes, you say—"

The dads shouted "Eyes!" and clapped their hands together.

I waited for an explanation, but didn't get one.

"And when I say ears," he continued, " you will give me your—"

"Ears!" they shouted, and clapped twice. A twist.

"And when I need your hands," the speaker commanded, "you will lend me your—"

You guessed it. "Hands!" They cheered, and clapped them together, thrice.

To ensure unity and compliance, the speaker made us repeat the drill. There was much clapping. There was much anatomy. Now I had a hangover to contend with, and an expanding list of body parts to declare, as well as a corresponding number of claps to memorize, all of this to be performed for the TV crews who came to uncover what it is we do here. It couldn't get worse.

"All right!" the speaker yelled. "Now I want to know what are we?"

"We're dads!"

"I said what are we?"

Welcome to Worseville.

The speaker laid into an inspirational opening anecdote. It was about the time, over ten years ago, when he was the only dad among the moms at the playground, and how he'd been shunned, or viewed with suspicion, and how that suspicion had intensified the day he sported the ugliest necktie to have ever juxtaposed colours and shapes. The tie—which he said could be better classified as a bib—was a gift from his son for Father's Day. How could he not wear it with pride to the swing set, as requested by the boy? J.M. Barrie was right at the end of *Peter Pan*. Children are gay, innocent and heartless.

But when the moms learned why this dad looked like a detergent box, they were charmed. By swallowing his pride he'd earned their acceptance. We've come a long way, he swelled. He told us his story, and urged us to be proud, and made us clap and name our body parts.

Though I couldn't identify with the worry addressed by his speech—the worry that some dads feel stigmatized for staying at home, or lesser and embarrassed in some way for having made that choice—I have to admit I was moved. I was moved by his story, and by his tie.

I had my own version of our speaker's tie. When shopping for Father's Day, Tracy noticed Tess reaching for a T-shirt on the rack. A pink shirt with a massive picture of an ant on it. It was in my luggage now, ready for another wear.

I also remember the day I was on the delivery end of such a gift. I remember my mother answering the phone in the kitchen that morning. I was about ten, and my younger brothers and sister and I were within earshot, playing at the table, making crafts. We had a box of scissors and paper and egg cartons and glue, and were occupied with the construction of caterpillars. By the way my mother answered the phone, I could tell my father was on the other end of the line, just getting off work.

Something happened. My mother sounded alarmed. "Why?" she repeated, and "How can they?" and "What are we going to do?" Then she said something about money. Other things were said in hushed tones. Then she hung up the phone, waited a beat, and snapped back into shape. She was her cheerful self again. Rory and Mykol were told to take turns with the glue.

Though I was only ten, I was the oldest, and that was old enough to infer what was going on in the adult world of our house. My dad had lost his job. I was terrified. I'd never known my mother to be worried before, or at least I'd never recognized it in her face and tone. My first glimpse of her fear infected me and grew. What would happen to us? How would we buy food? Do you need a job to keep your kids? I'd seen a thing or two on TV. People took children away from their parents sometimes. Usually they were poor kids.

That's when I saw that my brother Rory was about to cut into a fresh piece of red paper. I grabbed his hand and stopped him. When he tried again I snatched the scissors and gave him shit. Then I expanded my purview and made everybody stop cutting and pasting. My father was out of work. We needed the paper. My siblings were too young to understand, but I knew better. Uncut paper is worth more money. We had to conserve or die.

That piece of red paper was my ticket into the anxieties of an adult. It was, in hindsight, also one of the most loaded gifts I've given my parents. Such tokens accumulate in a family, such fucked-up and funny things. Together they compose the archaeology of our story. A kid offers his father metal clippings. Your ugly tie. Cough drops. My red paper. Their meanings devastate with so much love and good intention.

Maybe that's all any parent has for certain: to trust the meaning of what we offer, if we can't always guarantee our ability. One day our kids will come to see what we really meant. One day Tess will know I didn't ignore the little soccer ball she rolled to me. One day she will understand why I wouldn't take her to the playground by myself. One day she'll catch up and recognize not just what I did, but what I wanted to do.

When the opening speech was over, Dave asked which workshop I planned to attend.

"I dunno," I said, though I really meant, "I don't know the names of any."

"I'm going to the session for dads and daughters. I can guide you, if you wanna come."

Sounded perfect. While the session was, indeed, for dads who have daughters, the focus was anything but general. Half an hour later, three men—myself, a fellow from Omaha, and a student of French literature—stood at the front of a classroom, each with a mannequin head mounted on the table in front of us. These sported long, ratty wigs. We were demonstrating, for the edification of our audience, how to braid.

My challenge went beyond blindness. I have no hair. I don't even know how to comb the stuff, never mind how to part or bind it.

The man from Omaha quickly went to work, and though all reports agreed that his braid was wonky and frayed, he wasn't concerned.

"Well fine. It ain't perfect, but I don't care much 'cause she don't want this kind of braid, anyhow. I need to know how to French braid, and real bad."

The audience exploded with sympathy and horror. He was in the French braid stage of daughterhood. Apparently few dads survive. But the instructor expressed concern about us leaping ahead to the French braid. Knowing how to cut a steak is not sufficient credentials to perform open heart surgery.

"Just cut to the French braid," somebody called from the audience. Others agreed. This was not a class. This was crisis intervention.

By the end of our twenty-minute window, not one of us had successfully built a French braid. Worse, the instructor could see the collective despair and worry. With only several minutes remaining in our session, he improvised an alternative solution, and our only means to hope.

"Quickly gentlemen," he said, "first make a ponytail, then—"

We spent fifteen minutes on ponytails, and drove the workshop into overtime.

"I can't get all the damned hair to go in," said Mr. Omaha.

"Just tell her the leftovers are called bangs," I suggested. "Maybe she'll like them better."

I showed him how mine had bangs all around her neck and ears. She felt pretty.

The instructor grew frustrated. "Please, let's just say good enough. Now take the hair—"

I grabbed my mannequin daughter by the bangs.

"No, the actual ponytail. Grab it, and now flip it up and over and pull it through the hair just above the scrunchy, and down. Like so."

The instructor did whatever the hell he'd just said. It was met with a hushed awe.

"That's, like, pretty damned cool lookin,'" said Mr. Omaha.

"Fuck it," a dad concluded. "I'm doing that and telling her it's the New French braid."

A large crowd filed into the room for the next class. Only a few of my fellow braiders stayed put for whatever session was about to start. Sticking around seemed easiest, so I did. Maybe they'd give me a practice face and some experience with tweezers.

It was a solemn group. The crowd continued to swell. Extra chairs were sourced from other rooms.

The facilitator took his seat at the front, and calmly welcomed us to Anger Management.

That was enough for me. Role play couldn't be far behind. I needed an exit route.

Several obstacles blocked my escape. Most obvious was the thick crowd of men between me and the door. I also didn't know where the exit was. Less troubling, though no less real, would be the meaning of my quick departure. To up and flee at the announcement of anger management would mark me as a man deep in denial. Probably better just to ride this one out.

Our facilitator talked about the need for open communication in a marriage. He talked about the need to prioritize issues. He talked about relating as the basis of a relationship.

He talked about active listening. As he talked, he also proved that anger is one of the most boring things to talk about.

Then he canvassed us for confessionals. He asked a guy at the end of my row to begin. It was coming my way. I took a quick mental inventory. I tried to think of a scene in which I'd really lost my cool with Tess. It wasn't easy. My mind herked and jerked, like an engine that won't turn over. Just the idea of yelling at her was contrary to my physical being, and caused me to stop thinking about it, as if my brain had a safety switch that could power down my imagination. No question, I'd felt frustrated and tired when I couldn't soothe her, and sure I'd felt anxious when I couldn't do more for her, but angry? Nope. Or so I thought.

Most dads confessed to small things that ignited in them a disproportionate, though mostly benign, rage. One fella presented his situation this way. He might spend the entire day vacuuming, but his wife will come home and, without so much as a hello, notice a spot that he missed. That was it. Repeat several days a week, and you're here, in this workshop. To me it sounded more like a case of dust bunny, not anger, management. But there you go. Behold the trauma.

Yet by the crowd's outcry of support and identification, he seemed to have nailed some universal truth that had never before been expressed so succinctly. Angry men dust wrong, angry men dress their children wrong, angry men are not loved for their cooking. Angry men are angry and feel diminished, compromised and generally lacking. They also hate that stupid, dirty spot on the carpet, and their inability to see what she's talking about.

I squirmed as I listen to complaint after complaint. But as much as I wanted to set myself apart, I couldn't. Something was familiar. Every story was about deficiency. Amid the details of broken plates and primal scream therapy in the garage, I recognized some of myself. I knew deficiency, and its anger. At some level I was in Kansas because I was furious that I couldn't be all the fatherly things I asked of myself, or do all the fatherly things I expected. I sat with that anger for a moment too long, and my deepest contradiction surfaced.

I was a blind man trying to be a sighted dad. The one that my future had promised. The father I'd chased around a welding bench on the graveyard shift. And it hit me there, in my seat, like a Harley-Davidson: blindness had taken my father from me.

I followed the edges of my insight, feeling for definition. What did it mean to say blindness took my dad? Really it took the guidance of his fatherhood. I'd never let him or his model go. I wasn't just angry that I couldn't do everything for Tess, I was saddened that I couldn't give her what I'd known a father to be. My anger was actually, at its core, grief. The death of a boy's dream.

"There's some simple steps we can all take to own our anger, and to identify the sources within us," said the facilitator.

His first suggestion was that we make appointments with our spouses to openly discuss events that had hurt our feelings. Anger, according to him, is best dealt with on a schedule, but at a later date. His proposal left the crowd somewhat disappointed.

When he produced a contract that was to be signed by both partners, our Anger Management session dissolved into little more than clock watching. Maybe what some of us needed to get in touch with was a more old-school approach to anger management. They used to call it "repression."

I resolved to take something concrete home from my last workshop, something that I could lean on and trust to hold a privileged place in my new parenting toolbox. With it I would return home and continue, by trial and error, to fashion my own model of fatherhood.

Only one workshop had space left. The facilitator, Shirley, was an enthusiastic and loud woman with purpose. Organized, too. On each seat she'd placed a small bag of supplies with which we were to accomplish a task. To sew a button.

"A shank button!" Shirley corrected. "That littlebitty ring on the back makes it a shank button. You got a needle, you better know what you're poking. Am I right? Amen, I'm right."

She had a lovely, thick Southern accent, and a Baptist's oratory. She also had the demeanour of a drill sergeant.

"Now, first you will thread your needle—not your buddy's needle, not the needle of the man in front of you, I don't care how badly he—let me just give you the facts. When you are home alone with your needle and thread, you are ALONE!!"

I held my needle up and aimed some thread at it. Need I say more?

Next to me sat the hockey player whose kids chewed pucks. His elbow nudged my ribs. An intervention before my situation got out of control.

"You want me to do it for you?" he whispered. "I'll swap you mine when I'm done."

"No thanks," I said. "I'm gonna do this. I can do this."

I worked at my threading some more, but a blanket would have been just as likely to pass through the eye of my needle.

"What is this, gentlemen?" Shirley continued. Clearly she was holding up something for us to see. I imagined the head of a man who took a crack at his buddy's shank button.

"This here," Shirley explained, "is a good pair of shears. And let me ask you this: why am I here today?"

"To teach us how to sew?" Dave ventured.

"No! I am here today," Shirley preached, "because my momma said to me when I was a little girl, Shirley, where do I keep my good shears? Momma, I said, they're in your purse. And my momma said, and do you know why you are still alive, Shirley? Hmm? Because—you don't never go in my purse! That, gentleman, is why I am here today!"

Her speech was going directly in my parenting toolbox. Actually, now I wanted it to be a purse.

The hockey player next to me was still struggling. I, suddenly, was not.

"Did you do that?" he said.

"My God, I think so."

"I'll be damned," said the guy to my left. "Better not lose it."

I pulled out several feet of thread and cut it.

"No fucking way I'm gonna lose this," I said, and balled a massive knot on the end.

"Do not use more than eighteen inches of thread," Shirley yelled into the crowd. "It will get tangled and you will have to start over with your shank button!"

With my extra foot of thread I made a much, much bigger knot. The hockey player and several others tried closing their eyes. They theorized it might improve their chances of going home one day.

Sewing a button, I learned, is actually not that hard when you can't see. Yes, it was off-centre, and yes, it was loose and was anchored by a knot that could have been mistaken for a toupee, but my shank button was, indeed, attached. Shirley offered some criticism, but she couldn't deny me passage.

When I left the room, I think the hockey player was still stabbing at the air with his thread.

We celebrated the close of our conference that night with the culinary signature of our host city. A mess of barbecued ribs were served. I ate enough, as instructed, in order to achieve what are known as "the meat sweats." I felt awful, but I didn't care. My shank button was with me, in my pocket, and occasionally I flashed it to prove I'd passed Shirley's test. I was a capable dad. Tess could rupture buttons for the next twenty years, I'd be there. Maybe I'd wear steel-toed boots to augment the mystery of my power.

"So'd you get anything for your daughter?" Dave asked, piling another goopy carcass on my plate.

I said I'd give Tess my shank button when I got home. That, and this story. My work.

The Zoology of a Daycare

• • •

After a glorious year of soaking in spit-up and smelling of chicken purée, Tracy and I returned to wage work. Tess came along with me for the ride. At my university she began her studies in daycare. I'm serious. You too would consider noodling with paint and magnet tiles a curriculum when childcare fees are higher than the tuition for an undergraduate degree in physics. And you know what? It's been worth every dime. Tess was lucky enough to get the only available spot that semester. No, she didn't have to audition. No, we didn't have to endow the construction of a nap room. Years prior, months before our miscarriage, I'd added us to the childcare centre's throbbing wait list. Then I forgot to take us off.

Leaving our daughter for the first time with parenting surrogates is among the hardest things we've had to do. Without question she experienced nothing but fun and friends once she grew accustomed to the routine. Developmental benefits quickly became obvious, as well. Tess's motor skills and language bloomed because of the company and observation of other kids, and her immune system made contact with every virus and bacteria known to biological warfare. But a small, empty feeling roosted in me. It wasn't so much that I'd abandoned Tess, or sold her short by dropping her off for a day of bug analysis in the sandbox with her peers. Rather, a new awkwardness with my own time and sociability emerged. My day sucked. I didn't drop her off at daycare. She dropped me off at work. I wanted to go home.

That feeling arrived on my first morning back in the classroom.

"Uh, Mr. Knighton, sir," a student began as I set up shop.

Normally I wince at Mr. Knighton. Yeesh, I say, that's my father's name. This time, however, the formality made me sort of proud. Maybe I did, in fact, appear authentically dad-like now. Drool stains on shoulders are a dead giveaway.

"How can I help you?" I said.

"Sweet. Like, I'm enrolled in your class here because I have to take it, or whatever?"

"Sorry about that."

My mind shot to the daycare. What if Tess likes her teachers more than me?

"Anyways, I just wanted to like tell you that I'm gonna be on vacation for a couple of weeks."

"Oh." I thought maybe I'd heard him wrong. "Uh, so this is goodbye?"

"Can you just send me your notes and stuff?"

"To you on vacation?"

"No." He laughed. "Just like e-mail them when I get back is cool."

I did the math. The daycare teachers would spend more waking time with Tess each week than I would. My injustice nerve twitched. I was in this classroom to earn money to pay somebody to watch her so I could be in this classroom with—

"And, you know, the books?"

"I've heard of them, yes."

"Like, do we need to have those?"

I understood the painful new economy of life. Every moment at work was time taken from Tess. In my pre-Papa era, I would have indulged such a student's confusion with a helping of patience, and even amusement. Students are sort of charming when they're this lost to the world, or to the opportunities of the university. We're here to save hearts and minds. Now all I could think was, "I gave my daughter to strangers for you, and you're taking a vacation?"

A radioactive core threatens all working parents. It is a time bomb. If too much time is taken from our kids, we implode, and we may take you down with us. Even if you are on vacation, we'll find you, and exact our debt, swift and to the knife's point, then get ourselves home for tubby time. Careful. Snarky bus drivers, bank clerks, telemarketers, these could be parents who just lost a day with their baby. You could lose more if you rub them wrong.

When four o'clock rolled around, I couldn't wait to see Tess. I practically ran to the daycare and, as I've said, I don't run. One of my favourite pleasures remains that moment when I walk through the door and I hear her exclaim "Papa!" and bolt my way for a hug. Nothing like it in this world. Call it an addiction. I would almost be willing to leave her places just so I can come back and have her run into my arms.

I bumbled into the large playroom that contained all twelve of Tess's friends and classmates, ready to receive my daughter's grace. It came towards me, immediate and joyful, at the speed of first sight.

"Papa, Papa!" I heard her shout.

"Papapapa!" all her friends echoed.

I squatted down and opened my arms. Jackrabbit feet from across the room, then I felt a small and slender body slam into mine, its arms wrapping around my neck and squeezing with love. I returned the squeeze and told Tess how much I'd missed her.

Then Tess began to cry on the other side of the room.

The child in my arms suddenly felt unfamiliar. More slender than Tess, and taller, too.

"Hi Papa," the child cooed, and continued to hug me.

I'd embraced a little boy named Sumner. Tess shouted my name as if the word itself hurt. She was by the window, perhaps ready to launch herself in despair. My heart withered to a husk. The pain felt irreparable. Worse, I couldn't explain my mistake to Tess. I tried to as I let go of Sumner and chased my daughter for a make-up hug, but she couldn't understand why I'd chosen to give my affection to another child first. The gap between my blindness and her comprehension couldn't close fast enough.

I sat in a rocking chair and wrestled her to my lap. Sometimes the only way to make things better is to move on. We needed to fixate on something fun. Something new.

I pointed to a tattoo on my forearm.

"Hey, look! What's this, punkin?"

Sumner, already groping the picture, couldn't wait to answer.

"A birdie," he shouted.

Toddlers gathered. Swarmed, really.

"And what does a birdie say?" I asked Tess.

Older toddlers tweeted and cawed. The younger ones mimicked. Tess reminded the gathering crowd, with pride, "My papa, my papa!"

Parents arrived that day to find a dozen kids climbing up a blind man, squawking and roaring and fingering the pictures on his arms and shoulders. I became their illustrated farm and jungle.

All told, daycare wasn't as trying as I thought it would be. The time apart stung, but that tempered for all of us within a month or two. Parents naturally fret a great deal about the quality of their children's educations. We didn't. Tess learned songs, read stories, and picked huckleberries from the surrounding forest. Fire trucks visited for show and tell. Not even two years old, she came home one day with a bus transfer in her pocket, and shells from the beach. Paint, mud and leaves ringed her bathtub at night, as if she'd become some feral, Romantic artist. School was cool.

As for getting to school, maybe not always so cool.

Tracy dropped us each morning outside my office. In the parking lot she strapped Tess on my back and padded her inside a new-fangled carrier thing. Who knows what it was called, but it must have looked like a NASCAR roll cage. I loved it. Though designed for Tess's safety, it actually made me feel more secure. Should I plummet down a set of stairs or an elevator shaft, I could relax in the knowledge that Tess would simply experience my disaster as an extreme sport.

The only hitch was that Tess hated the backpack. You could tell. She straightened her legs so we couldn't lower her inside, meanwhile insisting—in her articulate manner of weepy, wordless protest—that she be carried in my arms like a normal kid. Or a grocery bag. Yes, her personality was emerging. She'll never utter the phrase, "Doesn't matter to me."

Because Tracy had to drive all the way back downtown to her office, Tess and I had to enjoy a slightly early arrival every day. We had half an hour together before the daycare opened. Lovely enough, and half an hour just happened to be how long it takes to get across campus at my speed. That's a hundred yards and several elevators.

Now, you've probably heard parents wish aloud that they had an extra arm. Wouldn't matter where evolution put it. Myself, I'd have cheerfully grown one from the back of my head. A fleshy ponytail, whatever, just so long as the thing could carry a few of the diapers, wipes, clothes, snacks and stuffed toys. Tess was even prone to bringing a shoehorn she particularly admired. But I needed that third arm even more than most parents because a white cane permanently occupies my right hand. Blindness, in this way, is sort of like an amputation on top of everything else. When caning with one hand and carrying Tess with the other, well, you can see the logistical problem. Just add to that all the extra crud a blind person has to lug around—my hotrod laptop, headphones, clunky audiobook boxes—and you can understand why blind parents should receive subsidized pack mules. That's how we started out at my office each morning, where I could at least shed a few pounds of stuff before we made our half-hour dash.

One day I put Tess down to open my office door and drop off my stuff. As her smear hustled about the hallway, I was struck by the marvellous and cruel quickening of time. In a matter of a few short weeks she'd taken to toddling on her own. The transformation could be measured in days, not months. I locked up and readied the roll cage for her reinsertion. When I bent down to scoop her up she made a babbling, tearful declaration of independence. She wanted to walk. She could do it herself.

I brimmed with pride, recognizing my own protests against helpful strangers. I also noticed the frightening quiet of Tess's footsteps. We needed bells. A suit of bells.

I threw her bag and empty roll cage over my shoulder. My hand clamped down on hers and we were off, the long pinball of father and daughter through the hallway, ambling to the elevator where I palmed the wall for a button. As we enjoyed this, our first toddle all the way to school, something in me shifted. I was stopped by a pleasant sorrow, and then a cutting thought. One day—and it will be in the window of one day—I will put Tess down on the ground for the last time. One day I won't get to carry her any more.

The miracle of her independence is as it should be, and we are among those in the fortune of having a little girl who can walk and grow in health. But it hurt to think of her no longer needing my one free arm. I tried to scoop her at the elevator, but she wormed in protest. Instead, the door opened, Tess walked herself on board and, as if to distract my attention, she poked the pretty red button on the bottom of the call panel. An alarm screamed through the building. Tess screamed in the elevator.

I punched buttons until the alarm died. Once again we were off. We said hello to every floor on the way down. I wonder how much of my life has been spent this way.

Onward we toddled out of the building. Already my body was growing more and more uncomfortable. My frame hunched to meet the height of Tess's hand. Her school bag and roll cage weighed me down in a contortion, like some fully equipped soldier at the end of a cross-country march. Tess enjoyed herself, though. Now that we were outside, she named the familiar elements of the world around her, such as tree, Papa, tree and tree.

Perhaps it was my delight in her words, or the distraction of my burning muscles, but I didn't notice that I'd stopped directing our progress. The guide became the guided. It's a blind habit. Even if a toddler takes my hand, I turn into a six-foot-tall wagon.

So Tess led us out of the building, zigzagged us down a concrete path into the woods, and kited my head into a metal pole. Her aim couldn't have been more accurate. My forehead was at the exact height of the pole's only button, and the blow from my skull set off its alarm. Unlike the elevator's, this one had pretensions to being an air raid siren.

I had no idea we had such poles on campus. They're for my safety. Should a student get a funny notion to molest me on my way to class, all I have to do is find this button, and its siren is supposed to scare them away. It worked on Tess. She dropped my hand and ran screaming.

"Hello?" a voice boomed from above.

I ignored it and called after Tess, trying to track her progress.

"Are you there? Hello?" the voice urged.

"Yes, hello," I answered the sky, irritated.

"Hello."

Tess's scream ran further away, but I was stuck greeting disembodied sky people.

"Everything okay?" the voice asked.

It belonged to a security guard on a two-way PA system.

That or an actual security guard perched in a tree, one who had a voice that sounded like a PA system. I ignored him and chased back and forth after Tess.

"Do you need assistance?" the voice tried again.

"No, everything's fine," I shouted back at the sky.

"Pardon me?"

He couldn't hear me over his own siren.

"She's—fine!"

Tess wailed.

"What was that?" the voice asked.

"Really, she's fine. Stop talking."

I called variations of "Don't move!" and "Come back!" The sky voice was not pleased by this.

"Security is on the way," it warned.

The banging of my cane must have sounded worrisome too, like the cracking of a whip, or the discharge of a small firearm.

Eventually I cornered Tess by a bush and calmed her down. She seemed happy to be scooped up for safekeeping. Her little arms clung to my neck as she whimpered and we walked through the rest of the wooded path, down several flights of concrete stairs and into our final stretch by the daycare's parking lot. The day's drizzle had turned into a heavy rain and we were soaked. We were still early, too. Nobody else seemed to be waiting for the daycare to open. No security guards hustled past in riot gear, either.

About twenty yards from the daycare's entrance, Tess used another one of her few words to name what she saw. Given our location in the foothills of the North Shore Mountains, it was a particularly notable word.

"Bear."

I froze.

"What was that, punkin?"

I scanned for a big black smear in the parking lot, and in the nearby trees. There was a garbage Dumpster somewhere around here. Somewhere.

"There?" I tried. "You mean we're going over there?"

"Bear, bear," she repeated, clear as day. Clear as a bear.

One of her little hands lifted from around my neck. I reached around for her arm, found it, and followed the direction. She was indeed pointing. Behind us.

I reeled around. The view looked the same. Still and blurry. The rain was loud, so I couldn't trust my ears. Smell? I smelled for bear. I have no idea what bear smell is.

Tess began to cry.

"It's okay, punkin. Let's just go over here."

I started to sprint, and hoped for the best. Within a few paces Tess grew significantly more upset, and leaned herself hard in the opposite direction.

"Bear! Bear!" she spazzed.

"Bear this way? Should we go that—? "Then it occurred to me. I felt her hands. Both were empty. One still pointed in the direction we'd come. Her pitch reached a level of toddler hysteria, more frustrated in tone than frightened.

"Did you carry your bear to school? Did you lose bear?"

She calmed a little, but whimpered "bear" as if, finally, I'd learned some basic English. I'd assumed her teddy bear was in her schoolbag, as always. Besides, black bears are as prone to visiting our campus as I am prone to expecting worst-case scenarios.

You might think her missing toy bear would be my permission to stop sweating. If so, then you have not had the experience of a toddler who has lost her security toy. Tess's teddy bear—known as, what else, Bear—slept beside her, ate beside her, watched reruns of *The Muppets* beside her, and, should all things continue as planned, Bear would have a seat at the head table of Tess's wedding, and would host Tess's faculty retirement from Stanford.

For now, though, Bear was lost in the woods somewhere between my office and this building. Where that might be, I had no idea. I can't even spot a real bear.

"I'm sorry, punkin, but I don't know where Bear is."

That was all she needed to hear. She cried an entirely new cry. It damaged my nervous system.

"But we can look, we can look," I quickly added. "Let's see if we can find her."

My ears still didn't detect a single footstep around us. There was nobody to call upon. No eyes to borrow.

"Tess, do you know where Bear is?" I asked. "Can you show Papa?"

She calmed. I could feel her head bobbing in the affirmative. Big sniffles.

"Good! Yes, you show Papa, okay?!"

Her head swayed back and forth in the negative. Then she seemed to be just bobbing it around for fun. My need was beyond her. Tess still had no concept of my blindness other than I needed my cane, although she still didn't understand why. One morning at daycare, as I unpacked her stuff, she'd run away with my stick, giggling. The laugh said it all. Papa can't leave without this. Why? Who cares. Papa can't leave, and, more importantly, now I have all the power of his stick. This is fun.

The only thing I could do was retrace our steps and swing my cane wide and near, like a metal detector, and hope for a soft, rain-soaked obstacle to get in the way. Failing that, Tess would just have to go into therapy.

We shuffled and swept, shuffled and swept, and all the while she demanded her AWOL bear. About twenty minutes later, back on our wooded path, her monologue stopped abruptly.

"Is Bear here?" I asked.

She giggled. Either bear was here, or she'd just found a pile of white canes beside a gang of blind people.

I stepped several paces ahead and she grew upset again. Back I went until she calmed. I tried another direction and she giggled until I must have gone too far, because she leaned the other way and protested.

I put her down and let her go. A few seconds later I could feel the damp spot where she pressed the plush bear against my shin.

"Good girl!" I cheered. "We did it!"

I bent down to pick her up. I hoped she'd let me, just one more time. She did.

After I dropped her at the daycare, I sauntered back to my office, ready to start my day, though it felt like I'd already lived several. The reception staff who work just down the hall from me had arrived, meanwhile, and greeted me on my return.

"Morning," I said.

"Lotta rain out there."

"Yep. Oh, and careful," one of them said. "There was a message about a black bear spotted on campus."

And Found

• • •

One Sunday evening, just before bed, it began to snow. Hard. When I stepped outside in the morning, ready to walk Cairo, the snow topped my boots. Even Cairo gave up. She held her ground in the doorway, certain she'd drown. I could hear cars slowly motoring along the main road two blocks over, but nothing moved on our unploughed sidestreet. We might be trapped. A family day in the snow. I went back inside.

"How bad is it?" Tracy called down from Tess's room. They were getting dressed.

"Pretty bad, but I can hear cars on First Avenue."

"Good," she said. "I've got a board meeting I can't miss."

"Thing is, I'm not sure we can get our car down our street. We may be stuck here today."

"It's okay, I can walk to the train or the bus."

That sounded fine, but she didn't add the part about how Tess and I would get to school. Without a car or driver we'd have to hike through the drifts to catch one bus, then hike for blocks just to get the second of three necessary buses. Who knew if they'd all be working, let alone hikable in between. No way was that possible in the snow with a white cane and bags and a toddler.

I'd grown to admire the daycare, and love what it gave Tess and what it meant to her. I'd also come to appreciate what it gave me as a father. Beyond time to write and time to think thoughts unrelated to parenting preoccupations, daycare saved us from my remaining major challenge. I had yet to take care of Tess on my own. I had yet to be left alone with her for a day.

I turned on the radio in the kitchen. The news reports confirmed that, miraculously, the university was open. That meant the daycare was open, too. My spine uncoiled a bit. All we had to do was get there.

"Maybe you and Tess will just have to stay home," Tracy called down the stairs.

She sounded nervous at the thought, but not unconvinced. Adrenaline sliced through me as if she'd just threatened bodily harm.

"Nope, nope," I rattled like a machine gun. "I'll dig the car out. It'll be fine."

Our neighbours Steve and Tat kept a snow shovel under their stairs, so I counted the hand railings between us and their door, then groped about until I found what felt like a shovel. Or a discarded protest sign. A quick press of the panic button on Tracy's fob told me which car to excavate.

A half hour later, I was done. I'd dug us down to the gravel and even cleared a path for us to drive into the street. This weather wasn't a potential day off. This was life and death. I was digging for my daughter.

We loaded up, got in the car, and Tracy pressed the gas. The tires spun, and caught. We were off. At the end of my little path we hit the street, where the car wedged its nose into a cloud of white, and stopped. Think of a cherry in whipped cream, and with as much likelihood of driving away. The immense snowdrift I'd thrown into the street held us hostage.

"This isn't going to work," Tracy said. "You and Tess should just—"

"Nope, nope," I rattled, and shot out of the car.

The street just needed some shovelling. Tracy's window opened.

"We're never going to make it to First Avenue, sweetie. You and Tess should just—"

I jumped on the hood of the car.

"I'm gonna bounce it. Just give it gas and it'll catch."

Another neighbour, Pam, asked if we needed help. Soon I had her bouncing with me. If the method worked, I reasoned, we could drive her as far as necessary, then let her dismount with enough cab fare to get home.

But bouncing didn't work.

Exhausted, Pam and I shoved the car back into its spot and Tracy released Tess from her car seat, into my care.

I will say this much before I let it go: stupid Canada and its stupid snow and stupid lack of municipal funding for goddamned snowploughs. It all added up to one thing: child endangerment.

This was it. My day had come. Standing in the doorway, I waved to Tracy as she began her long stumble to the downtown train. Tess sat perched in the crook of my arm, wailing with foresight. Halfway down the block, Tracy reiterated her confidence that we would be fine, and was gone.

I was confident, too. Confident that I'd already lost my cane, Tess's soother and maybe the dog.

"It's okay, punkin. We're going to have fun today," I chirped, then swooped Tess through the air. A little evidence never hurts.

Her demeanour settled as I shut the door behind us and lowered her to the floor. She stood there, still and quiet, as if planning all the things she wanted to do, and the order in which she intended to get away with them. Feed money to the dog? Insert cheese slices into the DVD player? Where to begin. So many things Mommy would prohibit, but Papa will allow, insofar as he won't know any better. I picked her back up, just in case.

"What should we do first, punkin? Want to watch a show? Want to play kitchen?"

Her diaper ballooned in the crook of my arm. It quickened to something I'd call critical capacity. Then she read my mind.

"Mommy?" she hoped.

Immediately another surge arrived in her pants. Something did not agree with her stomach. From all indications, just this one tectonic rumble might make up for all the diapers I'd never changed.

Afraid of a third surge, I loaded my free arm with rags, plastic bags, gloves and a towel from under the kitchen sink, and bolted upstairs. As we laid into major surgery on the change table in her room, Tess fussed and kicked, but also indulged a degree of curiosity in the spectacle of my efforts. Basically I had to imagine and to contain an expanding sea of effluence, and stay one step ahead of its physics, as well as those of a disintegrating diaper. Really, I had no idea what was happening, so I took extraordinary measures, walling

Tess inside a dam of towels, then propping her bum up on layers of fresh diapers, thus allowing me to attempt one and discard, attempt another and discard, an efficient infrastructure for yanking away fucked-up diaper after fucked-up diaper. Rags were deployed. Laundry filled one plastic bag, wipes and disposables choked another. A bucket of soapy water and even more towels were at the ready between my feet should a fresh insurgency beat me to the finish.

When I was finished I threw my hands in the air and declared, "Time!"

Tess stood up, cheerful as pie, a little girl ready for fun, and ballooned her diaper again.

We were out of supplies. I hadn't planned for this. And though I'd gotten her diaper on, or thereabouts, I can't say I'd gotten it on well. Leaks sprang. Her padding hung there like the billowy train of a wedding dress.

"Don't move, punkin," I said, with more wish than imperative. "Papa will be right back."

Back downstairs I raced for supplies, leaving her on the change table. Back up I raced before I'd made it to the kitchen, worried what might have happened to her high up on the change table while I was gone. She was still there, but digging into her diaper.

"Don't move," I reminded her. "Don't touch. Yucky."

Back I went downstairs. My hands palmed under the sink and through cluttered drawers for more bags and more rags. This time, when I returned to the change table, Tess wasn't there. She wasn't anywhere.

Everything seemed to smell, so I couldn't track her by nose. A few calls elicited no answer, either. My hands found no toddler on the couch, and no toddler in the bathroom.

The fantasy, of course, was that she'd run herself a tubby and was soaking with a good picture book. Around and around the rooms I went, hands out and groping for her like a zombie.

But in my haste, I forgot the golden rule of blind parenthood: never hurry. I am flat-out dangerous when I hurry. Tess might be fine, but I can come down on her like a runaway tank.

Turns out that she was standing quietly at the top of the stairs, where I'd left the gate open, and where I presently barrelled into her.

My arms shot out and snatched her from the air just before she tumbled down the steps, where the rags and bags went. In the same fluid motion I ran us down the stairs after them, as if to check that this was not an illusion, and that she was, yes, safely in my arms, not puddled on the landing.

I hugged her and apologized, and despite it all, she didn't cry. Not a peep. In fact, she was oddly mute.

I felt her hands. One of them held a small plastic bottle. The other hand clutched something she'd inserted between her teeth. A straw? Sort of. An eyedropper. Put that and a bottle together and you get Baby Tylenol. She'd found it on the dresser and opened it herself. The bottle was still full. Luckily she'd ignored the liquid, preferring the eye dropper's rubber reservoir. A prototype chewing gum, you might say.

The Tylenol came back into my possession, but she was not happy to relinquish her new habit. At least now I knew she was that tall, and had that much reach. I also now knew how fast an adult heart can beat without exploding.

Speaking of explosions, Tess's diaper expanded its form again.

I resurrected our towel and diaper show. Upon our second successful performance, Tess took it from the top. She wasn't sick or unhappy, not exactly, though she clearly felt restless and raw. All told, we completed eight rounds of diapers in less than two hours. The morning passed us by and we had yet to discover how we would actually spend our day.

She seemed to think begging would do. She enjoyed it so much, in fact, that she made me do it for the better part of an hour. I chased her around and around the house, pleading with her to drink some juice or milk or yogurt dregs. Hell, suck on a snowball. My treat. Anything, I just needed her to intake something moist before she withered up into a piece of baby leather. As I turned heel in the doorway, my foot glided on something soft. Something wet. A bit of something.

Yes, it was that.

Who knew how much of it had escaped, and where, and if Tess or I had been dragging it around the house. The whole area needed to be quarantined. I could never be certain if I'd cleaned it all up, or any of it. The situation forced me into my weakest position, without alternative.

"All righty, punkin," I said removing my socks. "That's it. We're going outside. Let's get your boots on and hope they're not backwards again."

The best strategy was some static play. My water bucket proved to be the handiest item ever manufactured. Out it came with us into our tiny front yard, along with a little hand shovel. The snow would be our sand, and keep us still and occupied till naptime. She dug holes in the drift by our steps, and kicked down little snow towers as I piled them for her pleasure. I have to admit, we had ourselves a time. The secret was to feed her a constant supply of activities, and thereby let me control, by my own invention, where she was at all times.

It worked, too, until she up and ran away.

The problem with outside, beyond wrestling a toddler by feel into snow pants and hat and gloves and boots, not to mention the further explosions that may erupt from way down deep beneath the geological layers of clothing, is that outside is just too damned big for me. To make matters more difficult, snow is a silenced world. It muffles all tiny footsteps.

I couldn't tell where she'd gone, or in which direction. Left down the sidewalk? Right? Into the street? Angling down the alley? No audible trace, no animated smear in the field of extra-blinding white. She was just gone.

Let me be absolutely clear about what happened next. I panicked. I panicked like I've never panicked before, and that's saying a lot. Every molecule commanded me to run, but I jerked with indecision on the spot. What if one direction took me further from her? What if I lost that bit of time? A neighbour. Was anybody home? Could I afford to wander in search of somebody? Puzzling over my next move cost even more time. If she was in the street, a car would have a hard time stopping.

For the next five minutes I hollered and begged and tempted the air with promises of cheese and goldfish crackers. No reply, no acknowledgement. Not even a giggle from the tickle of her new-found power. Not only did she have a five-minute head start on me in any direction, she also was clipping along faster than I could ever hope to move. I was profoundly alone, and growing more alone by the second.

Time curved as I paralyzed, shouted, and scanned our street. I reverted back to that kid who'd lost sight of his mom in a department store, and who glimpsed, for the first time in his life, the greatest unknown. A feeling of disorientation had ignited in me a permanent abandonment. Even after my mother found me five minutes later, the sensation lingered, took root, and grew over the years into my fear of death itself. Now I wanted to cry like that kid, the one who is certain he will live forever in aisle six with the Tupperware displays. His mortal cry. Children will be the death of us. Eventually I must lose Tess, and she, me.

But a hand took mine. A mitten.

"C'mon, Papa," she said.

And I was found.

My daughter tugged impatiently at my hand, wanting me to follow her.

"C'mon, c'mon," she said. She'd never said it before, but here it was. She'd come for me.

I scooped her up and hugged her, and she gave back nothing but the glorious preoccupation of a toddler who wants to continue her day.

Maybe she'd been standing behind me, or maybe she'd only wandered five, twenty or even a hundred feet before she returned for me, but I knew the real measure. It had taken us nearly two years to get here. What she'd found in the snow that afternoon was a new word, and its command. *C'mon.* It had budded from her lips, small and perfect. With it she'd save me. No, it wasn't her first word, but it was the right one, and it would be the first of many to come. The difference now? I could be lost. I could be blind, but she knew something about what I am. The guy you have to help along.

I remember standing on a dock with my dad when I was four years old. The place was Pender Harbour. A little cove in the Georgia Strait, off the Pacific Ocean. The occasion was a little fishing before supper. He and my mom had recently married, not that I really knew or understood any of that, but I did recognize that people had gathered here to celebrate something. I couldn't recall a time when this man hadn't been around.

Not much was happening on the dock. I absently reeled in my line.

"You know," he said, perhaps in response to something I'd said, or perhaps not, "you can call me Dad now. If you'd like to."

I focused on my fishing rod, uncertain what to say.

I only see it now. I was given something very powerful, but I didn't know exactly what at the time, or what it meant. My friend Dean had a dad. They lived upstairs and babysat me when my mom was at work. Dean used the word dad. I'd never used it. That's all I knew. There, on the dock, I remember it felt sort of dangerous, to be given a word.

We continued to fish in silence. I was scared. Scared to call him Dad. Because the word was new and powerful, I couldn't just accept it. What if it didn't work?

Maybe that's why I decided to test it, first. Standing there, casting my line, I waited out the silence long enough to make it seem like I'd moved on.

"Uh, Dad?" I finally said.

"Uh huh."

"What time is it, Dad?"

My dad answered. He told me, and I remember this clearest of all, that it was three-thirty. I had no idea what that meant, and couldn't have cared less. The word had worked. Above all, I'd felt its action. Words. They did stuff. Made things happen. I had a dad because I said so.

Now Tess and I had arrived at our own word. C'mon. With that, my daughter took my hand, and the faintest understanding of me. The smallest bit, just enough, of my blindness disappeared. I could let go a little. Even when the pictures of my memories go, the words will remain. Tess had given me one of those words. It bound us together a little closer, and told us that our world will grow clearer as we go. One step, one word at a time. It'll be okay.

And I know it will be, punkin. Hang on.

ACKNOWLEDGEMENTS

I am so very grateful to the following people, places and things for their respective contributions to this book, as well as my experience of fatherhood so far. Some listened, some read, some advised, some made our world what it was, but all said carry on in their own wonderful way.

My parents, Miles and Kathie; my siblings, Erin and Mykol; my other parents, Helen and Tony; Gavin and Ayden; Jen, Perry, Jack and Nate; our divine team at the Midwifery Group; the Capilano University Childcare Centre—in naps we trust; my colleagues at Capilano University; Wayde, Anne and baby Senna; our good doctor; our Cotton Lane neighbours and their open doors; Paul and Erin; Café Napoli; Scott and Indika; whoever invented the exercise ball; Jim Knipfel, for the encouragement and slapstick; Brian Fawcett and Stan Persky, who first convened my sentences; Susan Cartsonis; Doug Wright; Michael Goldenberg; Don McKellar; Richard Poplak; two Guinness per day; The Police for "Roxanne"—"It's funny!!" Tess says; my pals at Triptych Media; Mavis Arkinstall, we miss you; Norm and Gwen; Michelle Satter and all the beloved folks at the Sundance lab; Karina Vernon; socialized medicine; the Cran-Jeromes; Lola and Purdy; the dads of

Kansas City; Mariner; the soother known as "ish"; Robin and baby Liam; glass baby bottles; Karen MacCrimmon; Fratelli's fruit Danishes—breakfast of the underslept; Misty Rail and her wow big family; the Lavin Agency; white noise machines; parental leave employment benefits; the book *Healthy Sleep Habits, Happy Child*; and the BC Cancer Agency, for healing my gal.

This book owes much to the dedication and spirited advocacy of my agent, Denise Bukowski. I am grateful to her, as always.

To Jody Hotchkiss, I say onward, and thank you for the push. You have had a welcomed hand in the course of this household, and always have a spot at our table.

Thank you to Diane Martin and the folks at Knopf Canada for opening their doors to me and my family.

So much gratitude goes to Angelika Glover, my editor, whose patience, insight and encouragement made all the difference. If you don't have an editor, I highly recommend getting one. They're terrific. You just can't have mine.

Nothing in my world is possible without my gal, Tracy Rawa. Make no mistake, writing means nothing, and is nothing, without her. Every word is time she spent parenting without me. Her love and support is my home, and my fortune.

And, finally, thank you, Tess. Thank you for finding us. Mommy and Papa love you.

RYAN KNIGHTON is the author of the critically acclaimed *Cockeyed: A Memoir*, which was published around the world and is in development as a major motion picture. His comic essays have appeared in *Esquire*, the *New York Times*, the *Globe and Mail* and *Salon*. At the age of eighteen Knighton was diagnosed with the degenerative eye condition retinitis pigmentosa and is now blind, which is blinder than he'd like to admit. He teaches English at Capilano University and lives in East Vancouver with his wife and young daughter.